The Undying Self

Anthony Duart Maclean has been a teacher and seminar leader for the past 40 years. He specializes in stress reduction and increased well-being at all levels, with an emphasis on meditation, breathwork, Yoga and self-enquiry.

In 1974, Duart was recognized by the Maharishi Mahesh Yogi as a qualified teacher of the Transcendental Meditation technique.

Along with his life partner Lyse LeBeau, he is also the co-author of the book, *Awakening The Fire Within: Relationship, Leadership & Self-Esteem*.

Since 1994, Duart has been a devoted student of the teachings of the renowned sage, Ramana Maharshi (1879–1950). It is the wisdom and profundity of Sri Ramana that inspired Duart to write his second book, *The Undying Self: Vedic Wisdom in the New Millennium*.

The Undying Self

Vedic Wisdom
in the New Millennium

ANTHONY DUART MACLEAN

RUPA

Published by
Rupa Publications India Pvt. Ltd 2017
7/16, Ansari Road, Daryaganj
New Delhi 110002

Sales Centres:

Allahabad Bengaluru Chennai
Hyderabad Jaipur Kathmandu
Kolkata Mumbai

Copyright © Anthony Duart Maclean 2017
Published with special arrangement with the author.

The views and opinions expressed in this book are the author's own and the facts are as reported by him/her which have been verified to the extent possible, and the publishers are not in any way liable for the same.

All rights reserved.
No part of this publication may be reproduced, transmitted, or stored in a retrieval system, in any form or by any means, electronic, mechanical, photocopying, recording or otherwise, without the prior permission of the publisher.

ISBN: 978-81-291-4926-8

First impression 2017

10 9 8 7 6 5 4 3 2 1

This edition is for sale in the Indian subcontinent only.

This book is sold subject to the condition that it shall not,
by way of trade or otherwise, be lent, resold, hired out, or otherwise circulated,
without the publisher's prior consent, in any form of binding or cover
other than that in which it is published.

*This admittedly imperfect work is dedicated to
a perfected man of knowledge who
amongst all men past & present inspires,
guides & protects me beyond all measure.
He is
Sri Ramana Maharshi
The Sage of Arunachala
(1879–1950)*

CONTENTS

Foreword ... ix
Introduction ... xv

Part 1: Yoga and The Bliss of Being ... 1
India's Vedic Civilization ... 3
Key Concepts and Principles ... 7
India's Perennial Four Paths of Yoga ... 21
Vedanta ... 38

Part 2: Manifesto Spiritualis ... 49
Who Are We? ... 51
Being ... 68
The Human Condition ... 77
Enlightenment ... 86
The Man of Knowledge ... 95
The Essence of Spirituality ... 102
Our Description of The World ... 107
Countering Scientific Materialism ... 117
Power ... 127

The Primacy of Consciousness	133
Philosophy	138
Leadership	165
Society	169
Part 3: The Primacy of Consciousness	**173**
Bibliography	191

FOREWORD

Dr David Frawley
(Vamadeva Shastri)

The Primacy of the Self

Our true Self, being and nature is a state of pure awareness beyond our individualized body and mind, and also beyond all limitations of time, place, person, and action in the outer world. Though seemingly difficult to grasp, it abides at the core of awareness in our own hearts that embraces all existence as its own.

This true Self is largely unknown to us because of our attachment to our outer existence in the physical world. Yet, we all have a sense of it in the beauty, joy, wonder, and truth that flows through the special moments in life, and in the intuition of the eternal and the infinite that belongs to each one of us.

One of the greatest mysteries of life is that although all creatures are naturally born and die in the cycle of time, no one wants to die. We all have a longing, if not a vision, of our own immortality. But this immortality lies in our inner awareness, not in our outer identity. Discovering this requires a radical shift in how we perceive both ourselves and the world in which we live.

Vedantic Knowledge

Vedantic knowledge was a true revelation that Swami Vivekananda brought to the West in 1893, from which the modern global Yoga movement began. Yoga was an offshoot of a greater Vedantic knowledge. Yoga-Vedanta was the theme of early global gurus like Vivekananda. Vedantic knowledge is, simply speaking, the knowledge of our immortal Self that is common to all. In the broader sense, it is the knowledge of the Self that pervades the entire universe and whatever may be beyond it as well. Such practical Vedanta is the need of all humanity.

Vedic Knowledge

Vedic knowledge is the broader system of integral knowledge of Self and universe of which Vedanta is the summit. It reflects the pattern of knowledge in the Cosmic Mind in various mantric texts of great vibratory power and depth, which are called the Vedas. Vedic knowledge can teach us the secrets of nature relative to the nature of the worlds, their energies and ruling powers, types of creatures, how to live our lives, and how to work with the subtle energies of time and space.

◆

The author of the current book has presented the Vedantic knowledge in a fresh and direct manner that reflects the living experience of a seasoned *sadhak* who has an inner contact with the great gurus. It is no mere academic Vedanta that he presents, or a reformulation of the words of others. Through his insight, he can draw the reader into the experience of the true Self in a simple and immediate way.

Duart has also shown how Vedanta represents the deepest philosophy of humanity. Over the centuries, it has been reflected in various degrees and manners in the ideas of great thinkers across the world, including Europe. His book provides an excellent bridge between classical Vedanta and modern western thought.

The author's language is—one must recognize—dense and concentrated, much like the profound subject and the *sutra* or axiomatic approach of Vedic literature. His book requires a careful contemplation of every word and cannot simply be perused or quickly read. Each sentence can transform consciousness and is crucial to our ultimate well-being.

In addition to this, the author has drawn us through Vedantic knowledge into a profound examination of Yoga and Vedic knowledge as well. On such a Vedantic background, the true essence of these teachings is revealed.

Bhagavan Ramana Maharshi

Bhagavan Ramana Maharshi, perhaps the most recognized modern exponent of Vedantic knowledge, taught a simple and direct path of 'Self-being'. I would not use the term 'Self-realization' because the Self is always realized. Ramana instead shows us how to find our own Self-being that is beyond all dilemmas and dualities of the mind. Yet, we must also remember that however simply put, our inner Self is the supreme mystery, the ultimate Unknown, and that which is beyond all terms and ideas. Our true Self—the deepest core of our being—is that which is most secretive and most sacred. It requires surrendering of the mind and letting go of the known.

Today, particularly in the West, Ramana's profound teaching is being reduced by modern followers into some sort of pop psychology of instant enlightenment. Ramana's path, however, is one that requires a deep search within ourselves. This needs uninterrupted concentration in order to be accomplished. Duart's teaching reflects the sheer profundity of Ramana's true path.

To discover the Self, one must go beyond not only the ego of this birth but all attachments to embodied existence and the great *karmic* cycles of life. This is the supreme quest of all our souls. It is needless to say that Ramana is one of the great world gurus of this time and will remain so for centuries to come.

Yoga

Classical Yoga in essence is our return from the mind and its related ego and body-consciousness to the Self, the *Atman* or *Purusha*. That is the Self-aware universe and Self-being of all. The author directs us to the highest aspect of Yoga—Self-knowledge, though he also advocates the importance of all aspects of Yoga in the deeper search. Those who find value in any aspect of Yoga today should look into this higher Yoga of Self-awareness revealed by him.

Vedic Culture

Vedic culture or *Sanatana Dharma*, the Eternal way of Truth, reflects a cultural pursuit of Self-realization as the true purpose of human life, which also means incorporating the entire universe within ourselves. Vedic culture leads us to Yoga and Vedanta, but at the same time, it also provides a basis for these in a life that honours all aspects of the Divine presence in the universe—from aspects of nature to the forces and faculties of our own soul. Recognizing the restoration of such a Vedic culture is perhaps the most important project for humanity today.

Conclusion

Duart Maclean has produced the most remarkable compendium of insights that weave together the highest spiritual truths and most relevant factors of human life. The book is not just one single book but includes several. It contains more insights in a few pages than many books do in their entirety.

We ask the reader to take time with this important book, and to approach it as part of their own inner search that lasts a lifetime. The book is meant for a serious student of the higher truth who will certainly value its many treasures. One should live, meditate, and be one with this book. It will unfold a greater inner power and insight for all who attempt to understand it.

◆

Dr. David Frawley (Vamadeva Shastri) is one of the few Westerners ever recognized in India as a Vedacharya or teacher of the ancient Vedic wisdom. His field of study includes Yoga, Vedantic philosophy, Ayurvedic medicine, Tantra and Vedic astrology.

INTRODUCTION

The Limits to Thought

'Old men ought to be explorers
Here or there does not matter
We must be still and still moving
Into another intensity
For a further union, a deeper communion...
...In my end is my beginning.'
—East Coker, T.S. Eliot (1888–1965)

'Everywhere we remain unfree and chained to technology, whether we passionately affirm or deny it. But we are delivered over to it in the worst possible way when we regard it as something neutral; for this conception of it, to which today we particularly like to do homage, makes us utterly blind to the essence of technology.'
—The Question Concerning Technology,
Martin Heidegger (1889–1976)

Since the ancient Greeks, the West has given absolute pre-eminence to the intellect, which has produced science as its crowning glory. Through science, the intellect has opened new vistas and produced an astounding range of technologies. On the downside, the intellect has attained a cult-like status which often blinds us to other non-logical, non-scientific, yet valid possibilities—what we usually refer to as the right side of the brain. This has produced a dismissive attitude towards our intuitive side, which may contain the key to our very survival as a race. Science has neither liberated us from our relentless assaults on the environment nor has it reduced our violent tendencies towards our fellow humans, let alone other life forms. In fact, it has accelerated the rate of environmental destruction through technological innovation and amplified the scope of violence through increasingly sophisticated and deadly weaponry. This author is not an enemy of science, but simply a critic and a realist.

The Sanskrit term *Vedanta* means 'the end of knowledge' or approximately, the supreme Knowledge which cannot be surpassed. Such Knowledge is not empirical and cannot be known objectively. It is not the ordinary knowledge that falls within the scope of subject-object phenomena. It cannot be described with the help of language, as language itself is based on the subject-predicate structure of sentences. This alternate *Knowledge* (big 'K') is not a thing or an event which can be apprehended either directly or indirectly with the help of the senses, and it is therefore not a knowledge which falls within the immediate scope of science. Rather, it is a Knowledge which transcends speech and sense-data, and is therefore supra-mental or *ontological*.*

For the ordinary intellect, supra-mental knowledge is a mystery and thus the intellect tends to dismiss it as either useless speculation or wishful thinking or simply, escapism. Those, however, who have encountered this Knowledge directly and personally, understand that it is not something that can be simply dismissed as groundless. Since it is known directly—not

---

*Ontology (def.): study of the nature of being, becoming, existence, or reality.

in the way a subject knows an object but rather as an immediacy which embraces both the subject and the object within itself— and because those who claim to have discovered it are often individuals of great rationality and common sense, it warrants serious consideration from even the most sceptical of thinkers.

The British philosopher and novelist Aldous Huxley researched this alternative Knowledge and recorded his findings in his book *The Perennial Philosophy*. Huxley studied each of the world's major religious and spiritual traditions, analyzing the recorded experiences and observations of recognized saints, sages and mystics throughout history. He discovered that, in spite of linguistic, cultural and theological differences, the core experiences recorded by these exceptional men and women all pointed to a universal common denominator. This common denominator has been called: the Self, the *Atman*, Brahman, the Clear Void, Fullness, Awareness, Pure Consciousness, The One without a Second, Nirvana, Om, Pure Being, the Tao, the Spirit, the Naguel, the Holy Spirit, Infinity, Limitlessness, the Transcendental, the Immanent, the Source, Shiva-Sakti, Pure Intelligence, the Luminous, the Clear Light, the Hidden, the Dark Sea of Awareness, 'That', the Great, etc.

Those philosophers, given to precise definition of terms, empirical verifiability, rigorous logical analysis, etc. generally avoid even discussing these possibilities since the syntax and methodologies they use are hopelessly inadequate to either validate or disprove the reality of what these transcendental realizations refer to. Sri Ramana Maharshi, a modern sage of very clear, pragmatic thinking underscored the problem when he commented that philosophy ends where spirituality begins.

The ancient system of Yoga, dating back at least 5,000 years on the subcontinent of India, has always recognized the tenuous nature of the personal self and, by extension, the personal universe which has been built around it. Ramana Maharshi has commented extensively on the fleeting nature of the ego-self, describing it as merely a thought or feeling. According to Sri Ramana, the 'I'-thought is a fleeting shadow which seems to have substance when our attention is focused on an external object or an internal emotion, sensation or other idea.

Whenever, however, we attempt to turn our attention upon the 'I'-thought, the thought simply disappears and we find ourselves, for a moment, in a state of pure being where there is neither an 'I' nor an 'other'. He likens this to turning the beam of a flashlight upon a shadow in order to get a better view of it. When the beam is directed at the shadow, the shadow disappears, revealing what is truly there. Sri Ramana stated emphatically that the personal self has neither substance nor reality and through self-enquiry, we will come to understand—actually, know directly—our true Nature, which is not matter, energy, something or nothing.

According to the classical Indian system of non-dualism, known as Vedanta, the personal self along with its world view is a projection or superimposition on a screen of Being-Consciousness. It is this transcendental Self (not to be confused with the egoist small self) which is our true Nature. Since this higher Self of Being-Consciousness is not an object, nor is it susceptible to objective verification, it can be known only immediately and intuitively. This conveniently puts the Self out of the range of scientific proof, which always involves empirical verification. Scientific materialism cannot disprove the Self, yet neither can an illumined Sage prove the Self—at least according to the rules of scientific method. As Ramana Maharshi comments, the only way to know the Self, is to be the Self. In other words, it can be known privately, but not publicly.

It can be argued that in the absence of an object, the subject cannot know of its own existence. I know that I exist because I am looking at, thinking about or feeling something. Or to quote René Descartes, 'I think, therefore I am.' If there is no thing being experienced or thought of, then who, what and where am 'I'? The state of deep sleep appears to support this hypothesis because in sleep there is no object and no self-awareness. The subject requires an object in order to know of its own existence, even if that object is merely the thought, 'I exist'. Conversely, it is arguable that the existence of discrete objects demands a knowing subject. In the absence of a knower, can there be any objective, discrete thing such as a tree? A tree is a tree because a subject—someone—knows it as such. We talk about trees and rocks and human beings as we know them in our perception, but at the level of pure energy from which rocks, trees, humans and the space between them are ultimately composed, there is no such thing as discrete things.

Yogis who are advanced in their meditation practise gaining direct knowledge of the independence of Consciousness from its content when they arrive at a state of pure, empty Awareness. This state is called, in Sanskrit, *samadhi* (absorption). There are various levels of *samadhi*, but the penultimate level is known as *nirvikalpa samadhi* i.e. Consciousness without qualities or content. The emptiness of *nirvikalpa samadhi* is very different from the blank state induced by drugs, extreme fatigue or a severe blow to the head. There is nothing blank about *nirvikalpa samadhi*, since it is a state of intense and silent Self-awareness. Advanced meditators experience *nirvikalpa samadhi* in meditation but lose it while engaged in activity. When *nirvikalpa samadhi* becomes established not only during meditation but also during the three states of waking, sleeping and dreaming, the meditator has attained Self-realization. In Yoga parlance, this supreme attainment of the meditator is termed *sahaja nirvikalpa samadhi*, described as an effortless and natural abidance in the Self (Being-Consciousness).

For a Self-realized yogi, the Self and Consciousness are synonymous as well as continuous throughout the three states of waking, sleeping and dreaming. In *sahaja nirvikalpa Samadhi*, the yogi is permanently established in awareness of the world without forgetting his essential nature as pure Being-Consciousness. He has the direct intuition of the Self as Consciousness and of Consciousness as the Self. Those who have attained *sahaja nirvikalpa samadhi* simultaneously witness and engage themselves in activity. They lead ordinary lives and are often indistinguishable from the crowd. These Self-realized beings know themselves as a space of pure Consciousness, within which thoughts, feelings and other experiences rise and fall like waves, never leaving a trace in the form of stress or addictive behavioural patterns. They have attained total freedom and awareness. Such a yogi is considered to be a *jnani* (Sage).

Not only Yoga, which has its roots in the Veda, but also numerous other spiritual traditions recognize the Self as synonymous with pure Consciousness. Buddhism and Taoism are two other closely aligned systems. Furthermore, some of these traditions postulate non-duality as the basis of existence, otherness being a creation of the mind and not a true reflection of reality. They hold that there is a unitary Consciousness or Self (big 'S') common to all organic beings. The clearest and earliest expression of this notion is to be found in India's ancient Upanishads, a series of inspired works produced by numerous *rishis* (seers) over many centuries.

The Upanishads, collectively called Vedanta—meaning the end of knowledge—express the pinnacle of Vedic metaphysics. Being-Consciousness is the unifying principle that all species share, although the contents of Consciousness may vary from species to species, and individual to individual. Even though there is no doubt that worms have experiences different from humans, the two species share Consciousness and enjoy at least some capacity to experience the contents of Consciousness. Pure Consciousness, as understood in Vedanta, is not nothingness, emptiness or non-being, but rather, it is a vibrant, full Being—the very Source of the material Universe, immanent yet transcendent.

◆

This book, *The Undying Self*, comprises three parts, each of which is written in a style very different from the other two: Part I (Yoga and the Bliss of Being) gives a systematic presentation of the fundamentals of Yoga philosophy and is quite easy to understand. From there, Part II will be easier to grasp.

Part II (Manifesto Spiritualis) is the longest section, taking up about three-fourth of the text. It is a compilation of loosely connected topics, all of which are related to an understanding of the true nature of the Self. It is not a narrative, so the reader should feel free to open any page and begin reading. Some passages are lengthy, while many are short—usually one or two sentences. Part II should challenge the reader to reflect and look deeply.

The real value of this book will be for those who introspect and meditate on the topics that are being addressed. Also, the author does not intend to lecture or indoctrinate the reader, but rather tries to invite self-enquiry.

Part III (The Primacy Of Consciousness) is the final section. It is a short essay that I have included only as an option. Part III is an analysis of the relationship between experience and consciousness. It also addresses the scientific materialist view that consciousness is an epiphenomenon of biological processes—a questionable position that I do not accept. The topic is abstract and may not appeal to everyone. It will be of interest to those of a certain kind of temperament—one that is naturally attracted to analytic thinking. If the reader is not comfortable with analysis, he/she may feel free to skip this section.

PART 1

YOGA AND THE BLISS OF BEING
Overview of an Ancient System

1

INDIA'S VEDIC CIVILIZATION

'Totally windless, by itself, the One breathed; Beyond that, indeed, nothing whatever was.'
—*Hymn of Creation*, Rig Veda (1000 BC)

The Origins of Yoga

The subcontinent of ancient India was primarily an agrarian society made of small towns, villages and farms. Primitive tribes of hunters and foragers inhabited the remote regions. It was a diverse land of many kingdoms, people and languages. It was here that the timeless practice of Yoga began more than 5,000 years ago.

Modern India still reflects that ancient land, with the majority of her various peoples still living in rural villages and relying on agriculture as their main source of livelihood. Travelling in India today, one hears many different languages, notices a wide diversity of customs and cannot help but observe an array of different body types and skin colours in different regions. With a population of over one billion, modern India is the world's largest democracy.

In spite of huge demographic challenges and a history of being invaded and plundered and then assimilating her invaders, it is remarkable that India has not only held together as a democratic nation, but has advanced rapidly as an economic powerhouse within the global village.

The secret of India's strength and capacity to endure lies in her Vedic philosophy which goes back to at least 4000 BC. This open, tolerant and pluralistic spiritual system unfolded over the millennia and culminated in a series of inspired teachings known as the Upanishads. The principal Upanishads, which predate the birth of Christ, are of the nature of revelation rather than intellectual discourse and were intuitively heard by a series of inspired rishis (seers). What distinguishes the Upanishads from the antecedent Vedic faith which they form an integral part of, is their philosophical insight into the nature of Reality and their almost exclusive focus on the subject of enlightenment or Self-realization.

It was the great eighth century Sage, Adi Shankara, who wrote his famous commentaries on the principal Upanishads, establishing the non-dual nature of Reality. The core message of these ancient scriptures is that 'All is One' and that the perception of separateness is a mistake analogous to a mirage of water in a desert or to misperceiving a rope as a snake. They address the most relevant questions that each human being carries in his heart—'What am I?', 'Who am I?', 'Why am I here?', 'How do I overcome my fear of death?'. In every century, India has produced numerous Sages who have found, through their direct intuition and experience, the answers to these questions.

Ramana Maharshi, Nisargadatta Maharaj, Ramakrishna and Vivekananda are some of the more renowned masters who have appeared within the past one hundred and fifty years. Most of India's spiritual adepts, however, have come and gone quietly, largely unknown except to a few disciples and seekers.

Upanishadic wisdom finds its practical application in the

practice of Yoga. The Upanishads provide us with an inspiring vision of what is attainable by every human being, while Yoga gives us the means to realize it. The methods of Yoga are diverse and practised according to the temperament and maturity of the individual student. Each one of us has a unique personal and *karmic* history, as well as *svadharma* (physiology, capacity and life purpose), which means that no two students will follow the exact same path. Nevertheless, while the practices of Yoga are varied, their ultimate purpose is always the same, as is revealed in the word Yoga itself, which means to join, and to unite. The final purpose of Yoga in all its forms is to return us to wholeness and put an end to suffering.

Seekers and non-seekers take up the practice of Yoga for diverse reasons, such as improved fitness, better health, reduced stress, more energy, freedom from addictions, elimination of insomnia, better concentration, better memory, etc. In short, it is mostly for better mental, emotional and physical health. The list is long. However, the real underlying motivation for beginning Yoga practice is a deep and often unconscious impulse to return to the very Source of Consciousness and Existence: the unbounded, all-pervasive, immortal *Paramatman* (Self).

It is difficult to assess the antiquity of Yoga, but it can be safely said that it is very old. Over many centuries, various schools of Yoga evolved in different regions of the Indian subcontinent. Around the second century BC, a great Sage by the name of Patanjali synthesized and formulated various schools into a unified system known as royal (*raja*) or alternatively, eight-limbed (*astanga*) Yoga. In the centuries following Patanjali, his work, known as the *Yoga Sutras* came to be recognized as an authoritative text on the Yoga system. All competent modern teachers of Yoga recognize the *Yoga Sutras* as the key text of *raja* Yoga; they study and practise it.

The growing popularity of Yoga in the West has been focused primarily on just one of the eight limbs of *raja* Yoga, which is the postures (*asanas*). To a lesser extent, a second limb called *pranayama* (breath control), is often included along with the *asanas*. Four of the remaining six limbs refer to the stages of meditation. Meditation is also incorporated into current western Yoga practice, but much less frequently.

An ideal training in Yoga will integrate *asanas*, *pranayama* and meditation. It is equally important to gain knowledge through the study of key texts on Yoga, such as the Bhagavad Gita, the principal Upanishads and the *Yoga Sutras*. The best Yoga classes integrate breathing techniques, physical postures, deep meditation and knowledge into a seamless flow which may last up to an hour and a half or even longer. The greatest weakness of Yoga, as it is currently being taught in the West, is a lack of knowledge of Yoga's underlying spiritual and philosophical foundations; it is because of this that there is so much confusion as to what the term 'Yoga' actually signifies.

The two remaining limbs of *raja* Yoga address certain observances and ethics that students are encouraged to follow. The limb dealing with observances (*niyama*) enjoins the student to study sacred texts, to respect his or her teacher and to practise contentment in the face of adversity. The final limb dealing with ethics (*yama*) emphasizes on refraining from harmful behaviour, such as dishonesty, disloyalty and violence (*himsa*) towards other life forms.

The *Yoga Sutras* also encourage devotion to God (*Ishwara*), but it is not a prerequisite to the practice of Yoga. In fact, love for the Supreme Being unfolds naturally as a result of the awakening and purifying influence of Yoga practice.

Although most Westerners refer to *raja* Yoga when discussing their practice, it is in fact only one of the four major paths (*margas*) of Yoga traditionally recognized in Indian spiritual philosophy. These four paths are discussed in depth in one of the most important sacred texts of the *Sanatana Dharma*: the Bhagavad Gita ('The Song of God').

2

KEY CONCEPTS AND PRINCIPLES

'Whether pure or impure,
Whether all places are permeated by purity or impurity,
Whoever opens himself to the expanded vision of unbounded awareness, Gains inner and outer purity.'

—Garuḍa Purāṇa

It is well-recognized that a proper and comprehensive Yoga practice is a powerful ally in clearing our negative, often unconscious, behavioural patterns and transforming how we think about and perceive not only ourselves but also others. The practices of Yoga, principally the postures, breathing techniques and science of meditation are powerful engines for cleaning up our subconscious and becoming Self-aware.

Although the ultimate object of Yoga is Self-realization, the actual process of Yoga is one of self-healing at every level—psychological, physical, emotional and spiritual. Through regular and persistent practice, we strengthen our personal power and increase our self-esteem. As our false, negative and largely unconscious beliefs are gradually eliminated through Yoga, we become sane and whole again. Sanity, as defined in Yoga philosophy is our Natural State—the state of Self-realization—whereas ignorance of our true nature is considered a subnormal condition. The true purpose of life is to awaken from this self-created dream of suffering and death. It is not enough to merely understand our negative behavioural and thought patterns. Understanding is only the first step. We must also work to relinquish these harmful, often life-destroying ways of thinking and acting. Yoga masters never tire of repeating that Yoga is 90 per cent practice and only 10 per cent theory and concepts. This is why Yoga and its parent Hinduism is not a religion or theology, but rather a *Dharma* (Path; Natural Law).

The original texts of *Dharma* are collectively known as the Veda (Knowledge) and they are ancient. The term Hinduism is actually a misnomer—a tag applied by invading foreigners and not by Indians themselves. The correct name for what is called Hinduism is, in fact, *Sanatana Dharma* (The Natural, Ancient and Eternal Way). Yoga is about self-enquiry and direct experience; it is not dogma or a system of morality. Each person must know the truth about himself through immediate intuition. Philosophical speculation and scholarly disputes about the nature of cosmic and personal reality will get us nowhere. Accomplished yogis compare someone who does this to a donkey carrying a load of books.

Yoga philosophy and practice developed over thousands of years. It is an important and integral aspect of *Sanatana Dharma* and belongs to that rich and ageless tradition. The theoretical side of Yoga is not based on metaphysical speculation or intellectual analysis. Yoga theory developed out of the direct experience of yogis and *rishis* (seers) over many millennia. From their immediate realizations, rising from deep meditation and self-enquiry, they were able to articulate the structure and process of both personal and cosmic reality.

Yoga theory incorporates a deep grasp of the psychological

nature of the mind which is developed in the twin yogic notions of *samskaras* (impressions) and *vasanas* (mental tendencies). A basic understanding of the metaphysics and psychology of self-ignorance is essential for success on the path of self-knowledge. The following pages will provide a condensed overview of Yoga philosophy, as well as its practical application through postures, breathing, meditation and self-enquiry .

The Self (Ego) and the Self (*Paramatman*)

In the West, there is a tendency to confuse the term soul with the yogic term *Atman* or Self. Traditionally, westerners have always thought of the soul as a spirit that leaves the body at the moment of death and enters a heavenly or hellish plane of existence. Its counterpart, the Self, is regarded as the ego or personality. In modern times, these ideas are still prevalent, although there is growing awareness that there is more to us than only the body and the soul.

Soul, as it is generally understood in the West, is akin to the eastern view of a subtle body that breaks away from the gross body at the time of death and continues to work out its evolution on other planes. In Indian philosophy, the notion of the ego is referred to as *ahamkara* (literally 'I-maker') and is regarded as an unreal lower self. The real and higher Self of *Sanatana Dharma*, however, has a radically different connotation from either the soul or the ego-self as conceived in the West.

The Indian notion of the Self is fully developed in a collection of sacred teachings known as the Upanishads. These philosophically rich scriptures pre-date the Buddha (500 BC) and would have certainly had an influence on his thinking prior to his Enlightenment. The ancient *rishis* (seers), to whom the Upanishads were revealed in meditation, considered the Absolute to be *Sat* (Existence), *Chit* (Consciousness) and *Ananda* (Bliss).

From the limitless Power (*Shakti*) inherent in the Absolute, arises the Supreme Person (God) who in turn is the Lord of Creation and the father/mother of all that lives and breathes. At the core of both God (*Iswara*) and all living beings is the same Absolute—*Sat-Chit-Ananda*—and this Reality is not different from the Self (*Paramatman*). The Upanishads proclaim the view that Reality is one without a second and that, at the core, we too are that Reality—surface appearances notwithstanding.

To realize the Self then is to realize the foundational Reality of all that is as the very being of oneself. The Self is also called the Heart—not the physical heart, but the ultimate Source from which our life, body, thoughts, feelings, sensations, dreams, memories and even desires arise. When through ignorance of our real nature, the sense of 'I am' gets identified with the body and mind, we experience ourselves as separate from our surroundings and from our own Source.

This is the true cause of our loneliness, isolation, fear and low self-esteem. Returning to the Heart and realizing our identity with it is the only way to overcome death and put an end to our suffering. This is the final purpose of Yoga—Enlightenment.

Samskaras (Impressions) and *Vasanas* (Tendencies)

Dreaming is the realm of the subtle body. During sleep, the physical senses are not functioning, yet during our dreams, we see, hear, smell, taste and touch objects as vividly as when our senses are awake during our daily activities.

Our dreams are a mélange of stress release, memories, phantasms, desires, fears, premonitions, inner guidance and profound realizations. When we are awake, the laws of physicality and the operation of our five senses dominate our consciousness. However, the subtle body also exerts its influence on our daily thoughts, feelings and actions through the impressions (*samskaras*) and mental tendencies (*vasanas*) buried within it. These *samskaras* and *vasanas* together form the 'unseen hand' that guides the choices we make and the actions we conduct.

When someone feels impelled from within to do something he regrets, and that too against his better judgement, he says, 'The devil made me do it.' In this case, his devil is actually a mental tendency (*vasana*) residing in his subtle body that is powerfully exerting influence on his outward behaviour. Till we understand the role of *samskaras* and *vasanas* in our behavioural patterns, it is very difficult to bring about any real transformation in our lives and we will remain in mystery as to why we make the choices we end up making.

Samskaras are subtle imprints impressed on the mind as a result of our interactions with our environment. These imprints themselves are not memories; however, memories are made up of collections of such imprints. According to Yoga theory, our subtle body has incarnated onto the physical plane countless times, accumulating a huge number of *samskaras* which it carries forward from incarnation to incarnation. The mind can consciously remember only the most recent of these *samskaras*. However, the mass of older, buried *samskaras* also affects us at a subconscious level. When enough *samskaras* accumulate in a particular direction, they form a mental tendency called *vasana*.

Vasanas are the inclinations formed from our previous impressions (*samskaras*). The *vasanas* reside in the subtle body, and when the subtle body incarnates into a new physical body, it carries its *vasanas* with it. This is why a child is not born *tabula rasa*, but arrives with already established characteristics and a distinct mental predisposition. Some of these pre-established traits may not begin to manifest until later life, however, they reside latently within the psyche of the newly born infant like seeds awaiting the right moment to sprout.

Unlike *samskaras*, *vasanas* are relatively easier to identify as we need to only examine our behavioural and thought patterns to discover them. For example, if an individual soul has developed a taste for gambling during past lives through an accumulation of impressions associated with this type of activity, that soul will be reborn into a new body with a built-in mental tendency to gamble. Like a fertile seed, this *vasana* will require only the right set of circumstances to germinate.

In order to think, we must be conscious, but the underlying motivation behind our thinking is predominantly unconscious. Until we investigate what exactly is driving our thinking, we are at the effect of unconscious motivations. What most people do, however, is defend, justify and rationalize their thinking rather than investigate why they think in a particular way. For instance, bigots do not examine why they are bigots; instead, they justify their bigotry and stay bigots. Children are not born bigots, but may become so in later life. Racism is a good example of an activated *vasana*.

Our mental tendencies also create thought patterns (*vrittis*) in the mind. The predilections, prejudices and urges that make up our *vasanas* motivate the direction of our thinking and this in turn produces repetitive thought patterns. These *vrittis* form our attitude and character. Our thought patterns also lead to actions. We act because our *vrittis* tell us to act, thus producing further impressions (*samskaras*). The *vrittis* dictate what our actions will be in order to satisfy the urges and inclinations (*vasanas*) that gave rise to the *vrittis* in the first place. Our *vasanas* in turn are produced by collections of similar *samskaras* imposed on the mind by earlier actions.

From this, the innumerable vicious cycles that this process creates can easily be seen. Impressions produce tendencies, which produce thought patterns, which produce actions (*karmas*), which produce further impressions, thus giving birth to tendencies. This cycle has the unfortunate characteristic of reinforcing and adding mass to our negative behavioural patterns. Our unconscious patterns and negative ways of being in the world are all *vasanas*.

Becoming conscious of our *vasanas* and gradually erasing them through regular practice of yogic breathing, meditation, self-enquiry and other effective means available is the only way to break out of our self-created mental prison. Yoga philosophy considers this cycle of *samskaras-vasanas-vrittis-karmas* to be a beginning-less and an endless causal chain. We cannot stop this process, but we can step out of the cycle by realizing the deepest aspect of ourselves, the Self. Mental contact with the Self through meditation is pure, intuitive Knowledge (realization) and this direct knowledge is like a fire that burns the seeds of our *samskaras*, destroying their capacity to germinate and thus weakening and eventually erasing the *vasanas*.

The undying Self is the source and support of Creation, yet it remains untouched by Creation and its cycles. When we realize the Self, we are automatically released from the eternal chain of cause and effect.

Prana (Vital Force)

> *'The whole adventure of Yoga is but the play of pranic force...'*
> —Author unknown

Shakti, the Power inherent within the Absolute, manifests as *prana* (vital force). *Prana* is the totality of all energy that lies in the universe, including everything from heat, light, magnetism, electricity and gravitation to mental activity, emotions and every function of body and mind. *Prana* is also the bio-energy of all life forms. When *prana*—the bio-energy of the body—departs, the body dies. *Prana* is the primal force of the universe, extending from the subatomic to the galaxies and beyond. The molecules of water in an ocean are forms of *prana*, as are the waves that endlessly pass through that same body of water. Whatever exists is *prana*, whether subtle or gross, whether visible or invisible; all that appears relative and changing is a manifestation of the *shakti* inherent in the Self and therefore cannot exist apart from the Self.

Prana governs the breath and is the motor power of the

mind-stuff. For this reason, it has been said that he who knows the secret of *prana* knows the secret of Yoga. The breath is an external aspect or form of manifestation of *prana*—the life force that permeates and sustains all organisms. Blockages, stress, addictions, repressed emotions, etc. negatively influence the movement of *prana* in living systems. *Prana* is energy and energy can neither be created nor destroyed. But if its natural flow is obstructed, it will find another way to manifest. In humans, this can take the form of disease, mental illness, harmful behaviour and all internal conditions which undermine our well-being and happiness. The organism itself is *prana* and, as such, is governed by an evolutionary tendency inherent within all living systems.

This evolutionary tendency translates into the natural capacity of the organism to self-correct imbalances and to purify itself of all forms of toxic substance, whether material or psychic.

Of course, there are limits and if the system is subjected to a massive trauma or overwhelming stress, there will be a complete breakdown and the death of the body will occur. However, it is this evolutionary tendency, arising from the invincible power of *shakti*, that drives humans to survive, seek solutions to their problems and move in the direction of greater happiness, well-being and freedom. The timeless practice of Yoga is itself a product of this evolutionary force and is a collection of potent methodologies for eliminating obstacles to the natural flow of *prana* in the body-mind.

The techniques of *pranayama* (breath control) form a vital component of these methodologies. *Pranayama* is a means to regulate and direct the flow of *prana* through various breathing techniques. The immediate results of *pranayama* are increased emotional stability, deeper relaxation, inner clarity and ability to concentrate. All these benefits enhance the organism's capacity to self-purify. The system's resistance to disease is strengthened simply by amplifying the flow of oxygen to the brain, major organs, cells and bodily extremities.

Furthermore, the deep relaxation and mental calm that follows from the practice of *pranayama* facilitates the body's ability to dissolve stress and tension, thereby producing greater stability in the nervous system and a more relaxed supple body. These benefits strengthen the body's immune system. Regular practice of *pranayama* is also an effective way of managing alcohol and drug (both illegal and pharmacological) dependencies, as well as reducing panic attacks, depression and other psychosomatic problems.

Pranayama (Breath Control)

There are a wide variety of techniques of *pranayama*, and each one has its own specific benefits. Some of these techniques can be grouped according to similarity of method and results. The term *pranayama* is used here to describe a type of breathing process that incorporates some of the following characteristics:

- Connected circular breathing
- Inhale flowing into exhale, exhale flowing into inhale
- Breathing through both the nostrils
- Combining short, medium and long breaths
- Practising with or without *asanas* (postures)
- Practising sitting upright or lying down
- Variable practice periods from one minute to one hour

Two examples of *pranayama* practice:

1. Four short breaths followed by one long breath, repeated four times (1 min). It is a quick and effective pick-me-up.
2. Long, circular breaths with wave-like inhalation from the belly to the upper chest. It involves a relaxing release. The inhale and exhale are connected without pause for one and a half minutes, and it is very effective for stress management and stress release.

Pranayama strengthens the lungs and increases breathing capacity, contributing to better health and energy. There is a correlation between the fluidity of our breath and our physical and emotional well-being. When we are relaxed and centred, our breath is even, smooth and steady; when we are afraid, angry or tense, our breath is rough, irregular, laboured or suppressed. By working with our breath we will improve our mental, emotional and physical health. All forms of *pranayama* should be practised where there is plenty of fresh and clean air.

Physical toxins are released simply through improved breathing. The body eliminates about 70 per cent of its waste material through respiration, 20 per cent through the skin and 10 per cent through defaecation and urination. Healthy breathing techniques taught in Yoga may also benefit in the following conditions:

- asthma
- allergies
- high or low blood pressure
- insomnia
- stress-related heart conditions
- depression
- panic attacks
- hyperactivity
- chronic pain
- metabolic and endocrine imbalances

The following is a list of the other ways in which *pranayama* contributes to well-being:

- improves mental focus
- increases mindfulness
- generates internal heat
- oxygenates the blood
- reduces carbon dioxide in the lungs

- calms the nervous system
- revitalizes the entire system
- alleviates migraines and headaches
- improves alertness
- energizes the body
- improves digestion
- strengthens the immune system
- contributes to weight loss
- sharpens the senses
- reduces anxiety
- stimulates circulation

Pranayama is an effective practice for eliminating both physical and psychic toxins from our system. Experience with the more intense forms of *pranayama* has shown that it is an effective means for releasing suppressed emotions. These forms of *pranayama* are best observed under the guidance of an experienced practitioner whose presence will not only secure us but also provide us with additional methods, such as the use of affirmations to facilitate our healing. People suffering from depression and drug addiction also benefit greatly from *pranayama*, which opens the *nadis* (subtle nerves) and removes blockage to the energy flow in the body.

Chakras and the Subtle Body

Prana appears as both the gross physical body and the subtle etheric body, which comprise the totality of the organism. The breath is the link that binds the gross and subtle aspects of the organism together. With our final breath comes the death of the gross body but not of the etheric body, which continues its journey as a subtle manifestation of *prana*. Although the gross and subtle bodies appear to be distinct, there is an intimate relationship between the two. In fact, to some extent, these two bodies mirror each other. Wherever a group of nerves, arteries or veins interlace each other in the physical body, that point or centre is called a plexus. Similarly, there is a network of subtle nerves called *nadis* in the etheric body through which the subtle *prana* passes; wherever a group of these *nadis* interlace, that location is called a *chakra* (locus of consciousness and vital force). The etheric body with its *nadis* and *chakras* permeates the gross body and exerts a subtle yet important influence. Although the *chakras* are not perceivable by the gross senses, with practice, one will begin to feel them during *pranayama* and meditation.

There are seven major *chakras* associated with the physical body and they are located at the base of the spine, near the genitals, at the navel, near the heart, in the throat, in the centre of the forehead and at the crown of the head. These seven *chakras* are linked by a major *nadi* located within the centre of the spinal column called the *sushumna*. The *sushumna nadi* runs from the base of the spine to the head. *Kundalini* energy, which is another manifestation of *prana* within the subtle body, moves up the *sushumna nadi* as a result of spiritual practice. As the *kundalini* moves along the *sushumna*, it stimulates and awakens each *chakra* (centre of consciousness) in succession. Starting from the base of the spine, each successive *chakra* represents a more refined aspect of the subtle body. The awakening of each *chakra* reflects an evolution in individual consciousness. In descending order, the seven *chakras* are as follows:

7th	Crown *chakra*	centre for self-knowledge
6th	Third Eye *chakra*	centre for self-reflection
5th	Throat *chakra*	centre for self-expression
4th	Heart *chakra*	centre for self-acceptance
3rd	Power *chakra*	centre for self-definition
2nd	Spleen *chakra*	centre for self-gratification
1st	Root *chakra*	centre for self-preservation

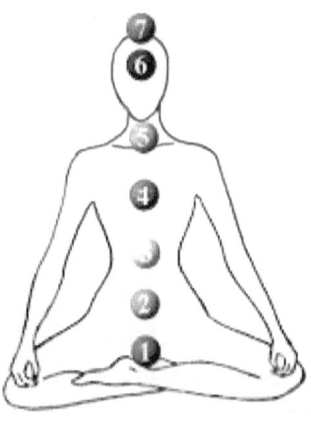

Chakras

According to traditional Yoga philosophy, when the serpentine *kundalini* energy reaches the seventh (crown) *chakra*, the yogi attains liberation (*moksha*). However, according to Ramana Maharshi, a highly regarded modern Sage, final liberation is attained with the final merging of the individual consciousness with the spiritual Heart, located, with reference to the body, on the right side of the chest. This spiritual Heart is not a *chakra*, but it is the Source from which the subtle body and each of the *chakras* arise and join what they ultimately merge into.

People interested in spirituality often confuse the subtle body with the Self, but this is incomplete knowledge. The subtle body, as well as the physical body, is pervaded by Self and arise from Self. However, the Self is in no way dependent on the subtle or gross bodies. The Self exists, with or without the adjuncts of the subtle and gross bodies. The real 'I am' is the Self, i.e. the 'I am that I am'. The gross and subtle body is also the self, but with a small 's'. The small self is fleeting, relative, prone to accidents and subject to decay. It is the mistaken notion that we are the relative body which is the source of our fear and misery. When we realize our true nature as the Self, we can still enjoy this relative universe but without the anxiety that arises from the dread of our own physical mortality. Who we truly are is immortal—beyond the laws of causality, time and space. Our true nature is Existence-Consciousness-Bliss (*Sat-Chit-Ananda*).

Paranormal Powers (*Siddhis*)

It is well-established in Yoga that there are techniques for developing extraordinary powers (*siddhis*). The Sages, however, have never encouraged their students to focus on attaining them. Instead, they have urged seekers to seize the opportunity of this incarnation to attain Self-realization. For them, the Self is Reality and to realize it is to realize our immortality. The body, being a form, is subject to the laws of time, space and causality. The Self, however, is the eternal Present and is the Source from which the impressions of time, space and causality manifest. To realize the Self is to transcend all limitations of relative existence.

Science itself is a *siddhi* that allows us to manipulate physical laws. Manipulating natural law, however, comes with a price as we have discovered with the advancement of science and technology. Every new invention creates a new set of problems that often outweigh the initial benefit. Nuclear energy is a good example. Genetic engineering is proving to be another.

For the Sages, going after *siddhis* is a lure of the ego that draws us away from our real purpose, which is to attain Liberation. Furthermore, whatever limited success we gain in pursuing *siddhis* will only reinforce egoism, which will in turn increase our thirst for power and control. The attraction of *siddhis* can also easily degenerate into black magic. Ramana Maharshi emphasized that the only *siddhi* worth attaining is Self-realization. He also acknowledged that those who Self-realize often find themselves bestowed with *siddhis* such as clairvoyance and precognition, but they come to them naturally as a bestowal of Grace. Moreover, being Self-realized, these egoless beings have no attachment to these powers and use them only for good.

3

INDIA'S PERENNIAL FOUR PATHS OF YOGA

'For all these Yogis, fearlessness, the removal of misery, knowledge of the Self, and everlasting peace are dependent on the control of the mind.'

—Gaudapada, (8th century AD)

Raja Yoga

This is the path of mind control—the Yoga of meditation. By bringing the breathing and thought processes under control, primarily through *asanas*, *pranayama* and meditation, the mind becomes completely quiescent and free of thoughts. This state should not be confused with sleep or trance, since the inner experience is one of intense awareness, deep peace and of being totally in the 'now'. When this experience is stabilized through repeated practice, the student is able to maintain an extraordinary yet natural, effortless and continuous state of complete Self-awareness through every moment of the three ordinary states of consciousness—waking, sleeping and dreaming. This state of

Self-realization is termed *moksha* (liberation).

Meditation is the key to success in *raja* Yoga. Yogic forms of meditation usually include the use of a *mantra* (sacred sound) which enables the student to focus his mind on a single point, gradually achieving a state of perfect concentration and equipoise. No longer disturbed by either extrinsic (e.g., noise, odours) or intrinsic (e.g., memories, desires) distractions, the mind naturally merges into its own source, the Self. This final step requires no conscious effort on the part of the student since the Self's blissful nature functions like a magnet for the mind, which at this stage has already been cleansed of its reactive conditioning. When the mind is ready, it is simply drawn into the Source from which it arose in the first place.

The successive and progressive stages of meditation make up the final four limbs of Patanjali's *Yoga Sutras*. These four stages are *pratyahara* (withdrawal of attention from sense objects), *dharana* (fixing attention on a single object, usually a *mantra*), *dhyana* (steady flow of attention towards the object of meditation), and *samadhi* (absorption, when mind merges into its source i.e. the Self). When the student is able to remain steadily and effortlessly absorbed in the Self and as the Self, even while his body is engaged in dynamic activity or deep sleep, he is considered Self-realized. At this stage, he knows himself only as the Self—his false, egoist identification with the body-mind is over.

The state of Self-realization is also termed as liberation or release from bondage. What is bondage? In Yoga philosophy, bondage is a condition of suffering which arises from ignorance of the Self. Due to illusion, we identify ourselves exclusively with the physical universe of time and space, external objects and events, and especially, our own body-mind. Since all that has form is inherently limited by that form as well as by the perceived limitations of time and space, identifying the 'I am' (*atman*) with the body immediately limits us to a particular form. Our identification of the 'I am' with this body-mind automatically creates the sense we are bound by time, space, circumstance and the physical laws which govern both the universe and our own physicality. It is this limiting identification which produces suffering. The body, as long as it lives, will always be bound, but does this mean that 'I' am bound? If 'I' means the body, then of course, 'I' am bound.

However, if my true Self—the 'I am that I am'—is something other than a physical form, something which both transcends and permeates the body-mind, then it is not bound. When the seeker realizes, through meditation and self-enquiry, that the true 'I am' is not limited to the body nor in anyway subject to the physical laws governing birth and death, then he realizes that he is inherently free. He recognizes that his feeling of bondage was a product of his own mind rather than an imposed reality over which he has no control. Once he awakens to who and what he truly is, the illusion of bondage falls away, as does his suffering.

Bhakti Yoga

The Yoga of Devotion (*bhakti*) emphasizes surrender to the will of God. Ardent love for the Creator and dedication of all actions to Him both purify the mind and open the Heart. Through devotion and surrender practised on a daily basis, comes the complete and final release into union with the Divine. Love for the Source of Creation develops spontaneously as a result of purification and surrender to the Higher Power. There is a strong element of *bhakti* inherent in each of the four paths of Yoga, since purification and a quest for the Source is inherent in each path.

Bhakti Yoga, however, focuses principally on the worship of and love for the personal God, and is mostly suited to those with a strong emotional nature. Sri Ramakrishna (1836–1886) was undoubtedly the most renowned *bhakta* in modern history with his intense and single-minded devotion to God in the form of the Divine Mother.

Karma Yoga

The Yoga of Action (*karma*) emphasizes selfless service as a path to the Divine. Working for the welfare of others and offering the fruits of labour to God is an exalted form of worship. Strictly speaking, all actions and their fruits must be offered to God on this path. This approach cultivates detachment and dispassion toward worldly things, equanimity in the face of hardship and setbacks, and supports the seeker in overcoming his egocentric tendencies. Mahatma Gandhi (1869–1948) was a *karma* yogi who dedicated his life to the welfare of the oppressed and downtrodden through his campaign of non-violent civil disobedience and his grass roots socio-economic programme for rural and village uplift.

Jnana Yoga

Usually referred to as Vedanta, the Yoga of Knowledge (*jnana*) focuses on the question 'Who am I?' The seeker meditates directly on the Self, understanding that to know the Self is to know the Supreme Reality in its essence. This is a path of discriminative wisdom which questions the real identity of the 'I' we unconsciously assume ourselves to be. Through self-enquiry into the true nature of the 'I', we discover that we are not the body-mind. In addition, we come to the direct realization that the Self, which is the Source of thought and the pure Consciousness underlying all experience, cannot also be an 'object' of thought. We can never know it as an objective reality, either intellectually or through the senses.

Thus, we cannot know the 'I am that I am' by means of intellectual analysis or scientific observation. We can only know it by being it. 'To know who you are, be who you are,' said Ramana Maharshi (1879–1950), modern India's most famous exponent of *jnana* Yoga and the philosophy of non-duality. This highly revered Sage has reinterpreted and rejuvenated the ancient practice of self-enquiry for modern times, making it accessible to all people, everywhere.

The Perennial Four Paths of Yoga Are One

Despite apparent differences among the various schools of Yoga, in essence, they are one. It is understood that on the road to freedom, every seeker inevitably will encounter and explore each of these paths. However, only one of the four Yogas will become his dominant path, depending on his individual temperament and capacity. Thus, Mahatma Gandhi was a *karma* yogi but also a great lover of God. He dedicated his life to serving the Supreme Being and he would consciously surrender the fruits of all his actions to the Lord. His last words, uttered at the moment of his assassination, were '*Rama, Rama, Rama*' ('God, God, God').

By comparison, Ramana Maharshi, who exemplified the path of *jnana* (knowledge), would arise each morning at 3:00 a.m. and prepare food for the many seekers who had come to sit in his presence, thus acting much as a *karma* yogi. Sri Ramana also insisted that the poor, who daily came to his ashram for a meal, be fed first and he unfailingly tended to the needs of the many animals, both wild and domestic, that sought his care and protection. He would be deeply moved, even to tears, whenever discussing the subject of God, thus also expressing the devotion of *bhakti* Yoga.

When any seeker, following any one of the four paths of Yoga, finally awakens to the reality of his innermost nature and attains Self-realization, he automatically exemplifies self-mastery (*raja*), devotion (*bhakti*), knowledge (*jnana*) and selfless action (*karma*). These attributes of mental poise, love, knowledge and selfless service are the untainted manifestations of the single source of all life. Each river on this planet follows its own unique course, yet each returns to the same ocean from which they all came, merging with and embodying the ocean's attributes. Likewise, when the seeker awakens to his oneness with his own source, he spontaneously embodies all divine qualities characterized by the various paths of Yoga.

The Eight Limbs of *Raja* Yoga

The classical *raja* Yoga of Patanjali is an integral and holistic system of self-mastery. It is holistic because it leads to a transformation at every level of our life—social, physical, emotional, mental and spiritual. It is integral because all of its eight limbs are interdependent and should be practised together to produce the result.

Most students of this path start with just one of the limbs—very often the *asanas* (postures)—and gradually incorporate the other seven. Our own inner inclinations, as well as circumstances, will determine where we start. For instance, we may have a back problem and a friend might suggest that the Yoga class she attends can help us overcome it. So, we may give it a try and join her at a local Yoga studio. Perhaps, we begin our practice with the twelve flowing movements of the Sun Salutation and observe an immediate benefit. The Sun Salutation is highly effective because it works with every major muscle group in the body, while simultaneously coordinating deep breathing with each of the twelve movements. We notice that our back pain has diminished and we feel physically better. We also feel calmer and more centred. We think that it is marvellous and start attending classes regularly. This is a common example of how people embark on the path of *raja* Yoga.

Others may start by signing up for a course in yogic meditation and discover the deep satisfaction of Self-communion and the inner peace that comes with it. Some will receive their introduction to Yoga through breathing exercises (*pranayama*) designed to reduce their stress and increase their experience of well-being.

Some might read a book on Yoga philosophy and find themselves encouraged to take up the practice. It really doesn't matter where we start since life itself will guide us when we are ready. Those who persist with Yoga will eventually incorporate all eight limbs into their practice. Like fingerprints, the path of Yoga is unique to each individual while at the same time, it rests on a common foundation of knowledge, principles and practice.

Let's take a closer look at each of the eight limbs of *raja* Yoga.

First Limb: Ethical Precepts (*Yama*)

Raja Yoga inculcates five ethical obligations that are considered essential to our progress on the path of Yoga. They are:

1. Non-violence (*ahimsa*)
2. Truthfulness
3. Not stealing
4. Responsible sexuality
5. Non-greediness

Since these ethical ideals comprise the first limb of Yoga, some teachers and seekers have said that the student cannot advance to the next limb until he is close to ethical perfection. This is a mistake, since any man or woman who has fully mastered these precepts will already be Self-realized or at least very close to it. They may have no real need to proceed with the following stages of Yoga. Therefore, we should not wait until we have mastered these five ethical principles to take up the other seven limbs. The various practices of each branch of Yoga purify the body-mind from stress and negative conditioning, thereby automatically strengthening the positive traits in our character and weakening our harmful tendencies. As we become more self-aware, we are able to check our negative tendencies before they manifest as destructive behaviour. Being more attuned to our true nature, we become increasingly unwilling to engage in activities which will hurt either others or ourselves.

However, understanding these five ethical perceptions and having a clear intention of following them is important. Choosing to indulge in negative behaviour while practising Yoga is counter-productive. Assuming responsibility for our actions and for the effect our behaviour has on our environment is the fastest way to progress. Avoiding responsibility makes about as much sense as washing our car and then speeding through the nearest mud puddle. It is equally important to not indulge in guilt whenever we slip ethically. Guilt is a major obstacle on the path of Self-realization.

Whenever we fall—and we will fall from time to time—instead of sinking into thoughts and feelings of guilt, we should have the choice to take responsibility for whatever damage we may have caused and make appropriate amends. Taking responsibility for our mistakes and correcting them is a sign of spiritual maturity. Cultivating this quality is the primary practice of the first limb of Yoga.

Second Limb: Observances (*Niyama*)

Raja Yoga urges us to consciously develop certain positive traits as a support to our practice. They are called observances (*niyama*) and there are five of them:

1. Purity (mental and physical)
2. Contentment (in pleasurable or painful circumstances)
3. Simplicity (moderation in all things)
4. Study (of sacred or inspired material)
5. Devotion to the Supreme Being

These observances are pillars that support both our Yoga practice and our daily life. They also are common to many spiritual traditions throughout the world.

Third Limb: Postures (*Asanas*)

Yoga is a process of self-culture that deals with the whole person. Although the Self is not the body or in any sense limited to the body, Yoga philosophy recognizes that a weak and diseased body can be an obstacle to Self-realization, especially on the path of *raja* Yoga. At this point, it should be emphasized that a healthy body is not a prerequisite to Self-realization since the Self is absolutely independent of the body.

On the contrary, it is the body-mind that is dependent upon the Self for its very existence. Throughout the millennia, seekers with serious physical handicaps and disabilities have attained the heights of Self-knowledge. Attaining Self-realization is primarily a function of intention, inner purity and Grace, not physical health or mental capacity.

Keeping the body healthy, clean and vital is the main objective of the *asanas*. Yoga postures keep our muscles supple and our spine elastic, increase our lung capacity and strengthen our internal organs. They also develop our mental faculties as well as bestow longevity. Illness puts us into a survival mode and takes up most of our attention, energy and financial resources. It also causes a blow to our self-confidence and reinforces our negative self-talk, especially when we are still ignorant of our true nature as the Self.

Keeping our body in good working order frees up our creative intelligence from attending strictly to basic survival needs. On the positive side, illness or injury will often mark the beginning of a transformation. Shakespeare wrote, 'Sweet are the uses of adversity.' For some people, a serious illness or personal disaster acts as a trigger for the complete letting go of the ego and a total surrender to the Supreme. There is no hard rule when it comes to Self-realization. It is a mistake to believe that only those with a healthy body and high intelligence can awaken—such a belief is rooted in ignorance and egoism, and is a barrier to liberation.

Taking up Yoga requires that we have a minimum amount of free time and energy to invest in our practice. The good news is that even a little bit of Yoga will take us a long way towards greater health, vitality and inner calm. The key to success in Yoga is not primarily the amount of time we devote to it, but rather how consistent we are in our practice. Just five minutes of *pranayama* combined with fifteen minutes of *asanas* practised daily will pay huge dividends.

The following six basic poses, combined with a simple breathing exercise and finishing with a few minutes of deep relaxation or meditation are easily learned and can be mastered by almost anyone, young or old. Some of the benefits of each pose are also listed.

A Twenty-minute Yoga Workout

Alternate Nostril Breathing (*pranayama*)—Four minutes (strengthens heart and lungs, improves digestion, purifies the nervous system, conserves energy)

Shoulder Stand (*sarvangasana*)—Two minutes (stretches neck and upper spine, improves thyroid and parathyroid functioning, reduces mental fatigue)

Forward Bend (*paschimothanasana*)—Two minutes (stretches entire back, strengthens abdominal organs, calms nervous system, reduces fat)

Cobra (*bhujangasana*)—Two minutes (strengthens back muscles, reduces menstrual pain and irregularity, relieves constipation)

Locust (*salabhasana*)—Two minutes (strengthens the abdomen, lower back and legs)

Hands To Feet (*pada hasthasana*)—Two minutes (improves digestion, increases flow of blood to brain, trims waist, stretches legs)

Triangle (*trikonasana*)—Two minutes (provides lateral stretch to spine, tones spinal nerves, improves digestion)

Final Relaxation (*savasana*)—Four minutes (replenishes energy, dissolves stress, lowers breath and pulse rates, relaxes entire system)

All of the above exercises can be easily learned in any beginner's Yoga class or from a good introductory Yoga audio-visual. A proper introduction to these poses from a competent instructor is recommended to maximize benefits and to avoid injury. This author would like to recommend an Indian yogi, Baba Ramdev, as a guide for Yoga practice. His videos and books can be purchased online and he teaches Yoga to thousands of students who are devoted to his methods.

The increased sense of well-being which the *asanas* produce provides a good foundation for meditation practice. Moreover, the *asanas*, combined with *pranayama*, produce a meditative state during the few minutes of final relaxation. This naturally induces inner repose which is carried over into the rest of our day. We are calmer, clearer, more centred and positive; our minds are tranquil, our bodies relaxed and our energies more focused on the tasks at hand.

It is also important to note that Yoga practice has tremendous therapeutic potential for those suffering from physical or mental disabilities or disease. Increasingly, doctors and therapists are sending their patients to Yoga classes to support the healing process. The combination of *asanas* and *pranayama* makes a powerful contribution to our well-being. It is not unusual for students to release suppressed emotions, especially during the period of final relaxation. Yoga instructors occasionally notice tears quietly flowing from closed eyes while students are resting on their backs during *savasana* (final relaxation).

This usually happens when they release pent-up emotional energy and often voluntarily report feeling lighter, freer and happier as a result. Since many stress specialists consider that as much as 60-80 per cent of all diseases are psychosomatic in origin, cleansing the emotional body clearly has a direct and positive effect on health.

Fourth Limb: *Pranayama* (Yogic Breathing)

Pranayama is also translated as breath control but this term can be misleading. There are numerous techniques of yogic breathing and each method produces unique results. The common purpose of all forms of *pranayama* is to return the mind, at will, to its primordial and natural state of silence. The legendary health benefits of *pranayama* are actually secondary to this primary purpose. Controlling the breath entails regulating the breathing process in specific ways in order to purify the nervous system and bring the mind to a state of equipoise. Yogic breathing leads to vigour, vitality and longevity and can play a major role in reducing or eradicating many types of illness.

The relationship between breathing and mind is very intimate. When the breathing is disturbed, so is the mind, and vice versa. Forms of *pranayama*, such as gentle alternate nostril breathing cause the breathing to become slower, smoother and subtler. As breathing quietens, so does the mind. If breathing becomes extremely slow and subtle, the mind also become silent and thought-free. Regular practice of *pranayama* will accomplish this. Alternatively, silencing the mind directly through meditation will have the spontaneous effect of slowing the breath. As thought processes diminish, breathing will become subtler, and if all thought stops during meditation, then breathing will become too subtle to notice.

To an observer, it will appear as if the meditator has stopped breathing entirely. In other words, the mind can return to its primordial silent state either through *pranayama* or meditation. *Raja* Yoga inculcates both *pranayama* and meditation as key practices on the path to Self-realization.

For beginners, emphasis is placed on *asanas* and *pranayama* as a means to bring the nervous and respiratory systems into a healthier and more relaxed condition. On this basis, the practice of meditation will then be smoother, easier and more profound.

Combining *asanas*, *pranayama* and meditation creates a powerful methodology for improving health, dissolving stress and inducing a state of deep restful alertness. The primary function of the *asanas* and *pranayama*, however, is to support the process of meditation.

Fifth Limb: *Pratyahara* (Withdrawal)

Pratyahara is the first stage of meditation. Normally, our attention is focused on objects external to ourselves. From the moment we wake up until we fall asleep at night, we are looking at, touching, hearing, etc. the items which make up our physical environment. We are also focused, to a large extent, on our own bodies, how we look, what we wear, etc. When the mind is functioning at a more subtle level, it is focused on internal objects such as thoughts, desires, memories, emotions and dreams.

Pratyahara is the conscious withdrawal of our attention from the external objects that our five senses perceive. Until this is accomplished, we cannot make the internal journey. How do we withdraw our attention from external objects which draw our minds like magnets? We accomplish this by refocusing our attention on an internal object such as the inflow and outflow of the breath or a *mantra* or the thought/feeling of 'I am' (self-enquiry). Unless we refocus on an internal object, it will be impossible to consciously withdraw attention from the objects of the senses. As soon as the attention is internalized through *pratyahara*, both body and mind begin to de-excite and a door opens to the next stage of meditation.

Sixth Limb: *Dharana* (Concentration)

Dharana means fixing the attention on an internal object and holding it there. This takes practice since the externalizing tendency of the mind constantly pulls the attention back to the external objects of sense. The pull of the senses is powerful for a couple of reasons. Firstly, we depend on our five senses for our survival. They protect us from danger and enable us to secure the basic necessities of life. Primal survival fears keep the mind focused on sensory data. Secondly, the senses bring us immediate pleasures and comforts that become habit-forming and addictive. These two factors set up a powerful outgoing tendency of the mind and inhibit introspection.

With *dharana*, the meditator practices returning his attention to the object of meditation whenever his mind wanders away. This is the principle of concentration. Concentration does not entail struggling with or overpowering the mind. Fighting against the mind's tendency to wander by using force to hold it in one place is the primary reason why people stop meditating. Forcing the mind doesn't work and is a form of repression that simply creates psychic distortion and psychosomatically induced illnesses.

Ahimsa (non-violence) is the guiding principle of Yoga and this applies equally to our treatment of other life forms as well as our own minds and bodies. Concentration does not mean struggling against the mind's tendency to wander, rather it means consistently and gently bringing the mind back to the object of meditation whenever we become aware that the mind is distracted.

The same principle applies to our goals in life. Forcing ourselves to fixate on our goals by the exclusion of all else produces an unnatural, even fanatical focus that creates stress both within ourselves and our environment. Concentrating upon a goal means simply bringing our attention back to it easily, effortlessly, without force or violence, whenever we become aware that we have been distracted with other matters. With practice, we become adept at focusing on our intentions in life while at the same time including whatever else is happening.

For instance, when a businessman is so concentrated on building his business that he ignores the needs of his wife and children, he is headed for disaster. He may get his successful business, but it will be at the cost of his family and, with his divorce, probably his bank account. If he is skilful, he will continually refocus on his business while simultaneously including both his family and all other matters with which he is personally involved. He will be one-pointed and relaxed simultaneously. This is *dharana* in action.

This approach to life may appear to be a long road to the accomplishment of our dreams, but in reality, it is the most efficient means since it avoids the stress and breakdowns that occur when we are too narrowly focused. Mastery of the process of *dharana* leads naturally to the next stage of meditation.

Seventh Limb: *Dhyana* (Meditation)

Dharana, the practice of continually bringing our attention back to the object of meditation whenever we become aware that it has wandered, leads to a deeper absorption called *dhyana*. For example, if we are meditating with a *mantra*, we begin to notice that the internal sound of the *mantra* is becoming increasingly subtle while the process simultaneously becomes easier. In *dhyana*, we find our attention flowing continuously and effortlessly towards the *mantra*, similar to the unbroken movement of a river flowing downwards to the ocean. This effortless and profound concentration is accompanied by an increasing awareness of space surrounding the *mantra*. In other words, accompanying the increasingly subtle concentration on the *mantra* is an unfolding awareness of Awareness itself—Awareness being the space within which all experiences arise.

This state of *dhyana* is blissful since the tension that is inherent within the 'subject (me)–object (*mantra*)' relationship is giving way to the merging of the mind with its object. At the same time, there is a growing sense of the limitlessness of Awareness and a palpable oceanic feeling of boundlessness that is delightful. On the other hand, in *dharana* (concentration), there is a sense that the ego-self is the active agent which is constantly bringing the attention back to the *mantra*. In *dhyana*, the apparent activity of the ego-self is taken over by a force from deep within, which pulls the attention inwards.

This force has often been called the Grace of God, or of the infinite Self, or of the Supreme Intelligence. For the meditator, all sense of doingness melts into a pervasive feeling of beingness as the process of meditation effortlessly continues to deepen. In the final stage of *dhyana*, there is a profound and blissful peace permeating the body-mind, and only the slightest hint of separation between the subject (me) and the object (*mantra*).

Eighth Limb: *Samadhi* (Absorption)

Dhyana ends with the complete merging of the subject (me) and object (*mantra*). When subject and object become one, both disappear. This is called the transcendental or fourth state. What is left is awareness of Awareness itself or the 'I am that I am'. The subject-object relationship of ego-self and *mantra* is a polarity in which each pole requires the other to exist. Without an object, there is no subject and without a subject, there is no object. It is the active mind that sustains this subject-object relationship. As the mind's activity becomes increasingly quiet and subtle during meditation, the process becomes correspondingly intimate and easy with the diminishing sense of distance between subject and object.

At the point where all mental activity ceases, both the ego-self and the *mantra* merge and vanish. This state is called *samadhi* (absorption) because the mind has become absorbed back into the source from which it arose in the first place, i.e. pure Consciousness.

Technically, this state is called *nirvikalpa* (without qualities) *samadhi* because it cannot be described. Since it is induced neither by drugs nor suggestion, this *samadhi* should not be confused with trance or hypnosis. Meditators who have entered *samadhi*—also called the fourth state of consciousness, since it is distinct from waking, dreaming and sleeping states—know that it is a natural state of full awareness and absolute inner silence. It is a condition of extraordinary alertness and at the same time, ease. When the meditator can enter the state of *nirvikalpa samadhi* effortlessly whenever he is moved to do so, then, it is called *sahaja nirvikalpa samadhi*, which means natural, effortless and continuous abidance by the self, as the Self. This is the state of Self-realization or liberation (*moksha*)—the supreme attainment of Yoga.

4

VEDANTA

Adi Shankara and Superimposition

An Indian sage once wrote, '...it is wrong to superimpose upon the subject...the attributes of the object and, conversely, to superimpose...[upon the object] the attributes of the subject.'

With these words, Adi Shankara (India, 8th century) pierced the Gordian knot of human misery. The primal cause of human suffering is a false superimposition of an object on the subject in the human mind. It is this fundamental confusion of the respective natures of subject and object which produces our personal anguish and anxiety, and by extension, our social tensions and conflicts.

Our knowledge of things is ultimately rooted in experience, and ordinary experience always involves an object or event as well as a subject. In order to make it easier to grasp the notion of superimposition, Adi Shankara gives an illustration using two objects, rather than the more difficult relation of subject and object. Adi Shankara defines superimposition as, 'The apparent presentation to consciousness, in the form of remembrance, of something previously observed in some other thing existing now.'

He demonstrates this false superimposition with the example

of a snake and a rope. A man on a road sees a snake coiled up and ready to strike. He jumps back in fear. He then peers through the evening gloom at the object of his fear and gives a sigh of relief when he realizes his mistake—the snake is merely a coiled piece of rope. He walks on.

The man had unconsciously superimposed on the rope his memory of a snake. All of this happened within his own consciousness although he was convinced the snake was real and external to himself. The phenomenon of superimposition creates illusions which can trigger a whole chain of events. In our example, the man's misperception triggered the emotion of fear and stopped him in his tracks. Other forms of superimposition can be more catastrophic, for instance, when a vengeful man murders an innocent person. In fact, a good case can be made that most human conflict, including war and genocide, is rooted in misperceptions arising from a false superimposition.

Regarding the more difficult matter of superimposition occurring between subject and object (as opposed to object and object), Adi Shankara affirms that it is natural for human beings to superimpose the qualities of the object on the subject. However, he also holds that this tendency is deeply flawed. The essence of his argument is that the subject can never become its own object and therefore can never have observable qualities. For example, the self as the subject cannot attribute a quality such as white skin or green eyes to itself, while observing its white skin or green eyes.

This would be tantamount to stating that my white skin is observing my white skin. In order for the subject to remain the subject, it cannot assume observable qualities, such as colour, taste, emotions, beliefs, size, location, etc. Once an observable quality has been assigned to the subject, the witnessing subject then becomes an object which is observable to itself, an impossibility, since this would require one subject which is the object and a second subject looking at the first while simultaneously being the first. In other words, the witness cannot witness the witness witnessing. Or, to give a more concrete example, the eye can see its reflection in a mirror, but without the mirror, the eye cannot see the eye, nor can the witness behind (so to speak) the physical eye see the witness.

It is true that common sense generally finds the subject/object relation acceptable with regard to other persons and things (e.g., I see that he is white, I pick up the vase, I smell perfume). However, the contradiction becomes obvious when a quality is assigned to the subjective self that is assigning it. When the 'I'-subject is turned into an 'I'-object, who then is the subject observing the object that 'I am'? How can the seer simultaneously see the seer seeing? Such a conundrum invites an infinite regression of witnessing subjects. In order to avoid this logical impasse, nothing empirical can be attributed to the original subject, which must remain quality-less.

Adi Shankara makes a clear distinction between the ego and the subject. The ego is a creation of the internal organ (mind), which involves memory, intellect, emotion, desire and conditioning, thus it (the ego) too stands as an object in relation to the witnessing subject. The Sage notes that human beings associate the ego with the self and, by extension, mistakenly associate this self with the subject. He points out that if the self is equated with the ego, then the self cannot be the true subject.

Step by step, Adi Shankara establishes that the subject is neither the ego, the self, the body nor the internal organ (mind). Through relentless analysis, he pushes us up against the question, 'What is this subject which knows, observes and witnesses all these gross and subtle phenomena—the self, the ego, thoughts, memories, feelings, urges, sensations, bodies, people, landscapes, planets, stars, the universe?' If the subject itself can never be observed or measured, then does it really exist? Is the subject real or is it merely fictitious? Or, if it does exist, is it simply not verifiable in the ways humans normally verify something? Is it a reality which cannot be tested through our normal channels of investigation, i.e. observation, analysis, deduction, inference, and the independent corroboration of others?

Having identified the virus at the root of the disease, Adi Shankara was able to identify and prescribe the cure. Travelling the length and breadth of India, this remarkable man discoursed and debated with the greatest philosophers and gurus of the land. The result was the profound spiritual regeneration of an ancient civilization. Shankara's genius has not dimmed with the passage of time and those who study his writings today are impressed by the depth, precision and originality of his thinking.

Philosophically, Shankara was not a sceptic, yet an important aspect of his genius was his ability to take the position of the sceptic. Shankara respected healthy scepticism, but was himself a master of the highest and oldest school of Yoga, the 'Yoga of Knowledge' (*jnana* Yoga).

Self-enquiry (*Atma Vichara*)—'Who Am I?'

> *'Shiva (God) is the Being assuming all forms and the Consciousness seeing them. That is to say, Shiva is the background underlying both the subject and the object. Everything has its being in Shiva and because of Shiva.'*
> —Sri Ramana Maharshi (1869–1950)

Self-enquiry has been called the *Maha Yoga* (Great Yoga) because it is a direct path to Self-realization. Self-enquiry deals head-on with the most fundamental philosophical and personal question we can raise, 'Who am I?' The practice of self-enquiry is very ancient and traditionally has been considered suitable only for those who have renounced everything in their one-pointed search for truth. In more recent times, Ramana Maharshi has revitalized this timeless path, making it accessible to all seekers, even those with busy lives and crammed agendas.

This method can be practised in a formal way by setting aside a certain period of time each day (for example, twenty minutes upon arising and twenty minutes before retiring) or it can be practised informally for a few minutes here and there as the opportunity or motivation presents itself. As we progress on this path, self-enquiry becomes an automatic process that continues unbroken throughout the day. It can be done while working or speaking, without reducing our ability to function efficiently.

For beginners, however, a fixed period of time set aside each day is recommended until the practice is firmly established. In order to experience anything—a tree, another human being, a desire, an emotion or a physical sensation—there first must be someone who is experiencing. Before we can know an 'it', 'he' or 'they', the 'I' must already be established. During deep sleep, there is no sense of 'I', nor is there any awareness of objects, whether subtle or gross. When we enter the dreamlike state, the sense of 'I' reappears, as do all the characters and objects of the dream experience. In other words, the second and third persons (you, he, it) cannot exist in the absence of the first person singular ('I'). The sense of 'I am' is the only stable aspect of experience, since the objects of experience themselves are continually changing. People, places and things come and go in our lives, but we remain. Our own bodies will change—sometimes drastically—but the 'I am' associated with our body will remain firm. This 'I am' is the only subject, whereas all else are objects. Even God is an object to the subject 'I am'.

Now the strange thing about human beings is our curiosity concerning nearly everything except ourselves. We devote our lives to understanding the world, God, the cosmos, atomic and subatomic realms, etc. but very few of us make a serious effort to examine the process of self-understanding. We ask endless questions about the nature of things, but we rarely question the questioner. Who is this questioner who wants to understand God and the universe? If we are ignorant about ourselves, then how can we be sure of our knowledge of anything else? Unless we know the subject, how can we claim to know the object?

If the world we see is basically a creation of our own way of thinking, asking and perceiving, doesn't it make more sense to first know the thinker, questioner and perceiver? Instead, what we do is assume that what we perceive is how the world actually is and then proceed to act on that assumption. As history reveals, this often leads to horrendous results. The philosopher Bertrand Russell, humorously illustrates this with a barnyard story. Each morning, at sunrise, a flock of chickens would run excitedly towards the friendly farmer who appeared with a bucket of chicken feed. This went on for many months. They were happy to feel so taken care of and well fed, and would look forward to the farmer's next visit. Then, one sunrise, the friendly farmer arrived as expected and they all ran to greet him. But this time, instead of carrying a bucket of feed, he was carrying an axe. And the rest, as we know, is history!

Sri Ramana Maharshi lived through the difficult period of the two world wars and the Great Depression. Westerners regularly came to visit him and many felt burdened with the cares of the world. They would ask him, 'How can we end war and bring about world peace?', 'How can we feed and uplift the hungry, depressed masses?', 'What is the future of the human race?', etc. Sri Ramana's reply was always the same, 'Why do you worry about world peace when you have not yet found peace within yourself? Why do you want to know about the future when you do not yet know the questioner in the present? First know whom it is that is asking the question and then see if the question is still there.'

Although Sri Ramana was mostly silent during his lifetime, whenever visitors would ask him sincere questions about the nature of the Self and their personal challenges, he would answer. Those, however, who asked questions out of mere curiosity or from a misplaced sense of responsibility, such as, 'What can we do to save the world?' would invariably be met with silence. Some found the Sage's reticence too uncomfortable and would leave, but many stayed and used the intense, pervading silence they felt in his proximity to look within. They would experience an inner revolution that transformed their lives.

In the method of self-enquiry, the enquirer is asked to seek the source of the 'I'-thought. This 'I'-thought is synonymous with the ego and is not the Self, who is pure Consciousness transcending all forms and substance. Nevertheless, the 'I'-thought arises from the Self and has its being in the Self. In the absence of the Self, there can be no 'I'-thought, since all thoughts—both positive or negative, true or false—require the light of Consciousness in order to appear. The Self is the Source that is Consciousness. In fact, all phenomena—from atoms to galaxies—appear by virtue of the borrowed light of the intelligent Self.

The 'I'-thought always takes the form of some limiting identification, which is invariably the 'I-am-the-body' idea. The 'I-am-the-body' idea is not exactly false but neither is it true, and this is the cause of our worries, fears and tensions. It is also the root cause of our aggression in all its ugly forms. The body is certainly the vehicle through which the Self finds expression in this realm of existence. In this sense, the 'I-am-the-body' idea is correct.

However, it is false when the Self is considered to be limited to, or in any way, dependent upon the body. For one thing, the body is mortal, whereas the Self is immortal and untouched either by the creation or dissolution of the organism. Furthermore, the laws of time and space condition and determine the destiny of the body, whereas the Self stands aloof from these limiting factors. In other words, the body is inescapably mortal and bound, whereas the Self is inherently immortal and free. Self-realization simply entails awakening to the reality that who we are is the all-inclusive Self and not merely the physical body or some subtle etheric substance inhabiting the body.

This is the final conclusion of two great Sages—Adi Shankara and Sri Ramana Maharshi. This awakening to the Self is not something conceptual. It comes with letting go of our limited and erroneous notions of what we are and a complete surrender of our egoistic tendencies. Such a transformation is a complete internal revolution, which touches every fibre of our being; it cannot be obtained by reading books, although books can be useful allies on the path.

It also cannot be reached by changing the external circumstances of our life. Abandoning our families or quitting our jobs to lead a monastic life is unnecessary because the real work is entirely internal. The philosophy underpinning the process of self-enquiry says, 'You are already the Self, all you need to do is let go of the idea that you are something other.' By tracing the 'I'-thought—which is a limited sense of self—back to its source, we realize the truth of our being. This does not require changing our religion or adopting a religion or dropping our duties and responsibilities. It does, however, mean a consistent and committed inner quest to discover the Self. It is work that no one can do for us. There is no higher power that can save us, for in reality, we are that higher power we seek and are fully capable of our own salvation.

There are a couple of ways of practising self-enquiry. One way is to dwell on the sense of 'I am' constantly. Nisargadatta Maharaj, a younger contemporary of Sri Ramana Maharshi, taught this method. *Aham-bhava* is the Sanskrit term for the sense or feeling of 'I am'. This feeling of 'I am' is subtler than thoughts, emotions or body awareness.

Aham-bhava is subtle like space and with practice, the conscious mind will become aware of it. The feeling of *aham-bhava* is always there, but because the mind is habitually focused on external sensations, objects and mental projections such as thoughts, memories and desires, we are unaware of it. By turning the attention inward—away from sense objects, desires, emotions and even thoughts—we become aware of this subtle feeling of our own existence—the 'I am' (*atman*).

Sri Ramana encouraged seekers to turn their attention inwards by actually looking for the 'I'-thought and seeing if they could find it. By actively looking for the 'I'-thought, the attention is automatically withdrawn from sense objects, desires, etc. and directed inwards. The mind, however, will not be able to find the 'I'-thought, which is like a fleeting shadow that disappears the moment the light of awareness is focused on it. In this single movement of the mind towards the 'I'-thought, both the external world and the 'I'-thought itself will vanish, allowing the pure Self—the 'I am'—to flash forth as an intense silent Awareness free of thought and all other phenomena.

Generally, Sri Ramana recommended the following method, which can be practised by either sitting quietly or while involved in normal activities. Start by observing the mind and its contents. Whatever is momentarily present in consciousness, whether a thought, emotion or desire, etc., silently ask the following question, 'For whom is this thought (emotion, etc.)?' The natural unspoken response will be, 'For me.' Then, ask silently, 'Who am I?' At this point, either search for the 'I'-thought, as previously suggested, or put the attention directly on to the feeling of 'I am' (*aham-bhava*).

In either of the cases, the mind will momentarily merge into the source from which it originally arose, i.e. the Self. With practice, this merging will lengthen and returning the mind to its Source will become increasingly easy and natural. It should be noted that the question, 'Who am I?' does not call for an intellectual response. The self-enquiry is not an intellectual process; rather it is seeking for the very Source of the intellect itself. Self-enquiry is not analysis; it is surrendering of the intellect to the Self and a merging of the mind into the Heart.

For those who found the direct method of self-enquiry too challenging, Sri Ramana would sometimes suggest alternatives, such as meditating with a *mantra*. Accordingly, he offered the following approach, in his own words:

'Among the many names of God, no name suits God, who

abides in the Heart, devoid of thought, so truly, aptly, and beautifully as the name 'I' or 'I am' (aham). Of all the known names of God, the name of God, 'aham–aham', alone will resound triumphantly when the ego is destroyed, rising as the silent Supreme Word (mouna-para-vak) in the Heart-space of those whose attention is Selfward-facing. Even if one unceasingly meditates upon that name, 'I–I', with one's attention on the feeling 'I am' (aham), it will take one and plunge it into the source from which the thought arises, destroying the ego...'

Self-enquiry weakens and destroys the *samskaras* (impressions) which form the basis of our patterns (*vasanas*) and negative conditioning. On this path of Self-knowledge (*jnana*), the direct intuition of the Self is a liberating insight, which like fire, burns the seeds of our *samskaras* and destroys their capacity to germinate as patterns. The method of self-enquiry is a potent weapon which, along with breathing and other practices of Yoga, enables us to overcome our patterns and negative self-concept, strengthens our self-esteem and personal power, and ultimately, brings us to full awakening in the Self.

India's Perennial Yoga-Vedanta In The New Millennium

> *'He has perfect Wisdom who is a yogi firmly established in non- duality...'*
>
> —Atma Sakshatkara, The Agamas

> *'The state of rest that shines when all desire has ceased is the powerful experience of Vedanta.'*
> —Sri Muruganar (1893–1973)

Yoga-Vedanta began to take roots in the West at the end of the nineteenth century. Its influence has grown steadily in the past one hundred years and shows no signs of abating. In fact, interest in this ancient and time-tested methodology is accelerating not only in the West but also throughout the world, including the Middle East and the Far East. Increasing disillusionment with the world's traditional religions has created a spiritual vacuum that the human spirit longs to fill. Yoga, which is an integral aspect of *Sanatana Dharma*, is a scientific and rationalistic approach to Self-knowledge and inner peace, and is free from the dogmatism and leaps of faith often required in traditional religion. The benefits of Yoga are being verified scientifically for everyone to see. These benefits, which can be directly experienced by anyone who even briefly takes up the practice, are responsible for the universal appeal of Yoga.

Additionally, Yoga does not call for anyone to change their religion or adopt other cultural traits. Yoga can be integrated into the spiritual practices of people of all faiths and philosophies, so long as those systems are not extremist or reactionary. An open mind and a commitment to the highest power in oneself are the only prerequisites. Having said this, it must be emphasized that the ancient science of Yoga has its roots and its very being in the Original Knowledge, i.e. the Veda-Vedanta, of the *Sanatana Dharma*.

Any attempt to disconnect Yoga from its source and to claim that it is independent of its roots destroys the very spirit of Yoga and reduces it to a fitness program lacking spirituality. When Yoga becomes a toy of the separating self-aggrandizing ego, its true meaning is lost and is no longer Yoga (union).

Yoga is a divine offering to all humanity. In a world that is currently confronted by turmoil and uncertainty on so many fronts, Yoga offers a healing light to one and all. Our world is rapidly moving through a period of profound change. The author believes that in spite of present difficulties, the Sun of enlightenment is steadily rising on the horizon and a new day is about to begin.

PART 2

MANIFESTO SPIRITUALIS
A Pithy Compilation from the Edge

1

WHO ARE WE?
Consciousness and the Self

'Weapons cannot cut It; fire cannot burn It; water cannot wet It; wind cannot dry It.'

—The Bhagavad Gita

We are the Self; we are Consciousness. The Self is pure Consciousness. All we ever witness, hear or touch is the power of pure Consciousness. This world, which to our senses, appears as an infinite number of objects separated by time and space, is merely a mass of energy. The universe itself is a mass of energy. Name and form, i.e. 'material objects', are creations of our mind; the Reality is quite different. The Indian Sages call this energy *Shakti*, or alternatively, *prana*. In general, *prana* is the term used for the energy or 'vital force' inhabiting organic beings. Energy, *Shakti*, *prana*—all these terms denote power. Power is not a 'thing', although to our limited senses, it may appear as a 'thing'. These appearances do not convey the reality that all we are witnessing is simply manifestations of power and that whatever discreteness we believe we are observing is simply not so.

There is no such thing as definitive discreteness anywhere in the universe; there is only power, and this power has its being in Consciousness. In short, everything we know is some form of appearance. In fact, all experiences are appearances, including sensory experience and abstract thinking. The physical world we believe we know has its being in Consciousness first, and then in matter—that too, inferentially.

In the absence of Consciousness, there is nothing; there is neither existence nor non-existence, there is neither fullness nor void. Everything depends on Consciousness. In the absence of Consciousness, there can be no afterlife. In the absence of Consciousness, God cannot know Himself, the Devil cannot know himself, the angels and the demons cannot know themselves. Even the animals, birds, fish, insects, plants or microbes cannot know themselves.

What has just been written is undeniable. For whatever lives, all experiences—from the microscopic to the macrocosmic—is an appearance, and appearance is absolutely dependent on Consciousness. When Jesus Christ was being crucified, all that he saw, felt and thought about were appearances in Consciousness. Even his realization that he was a Son of God was an appearance appearing in Consciousness. The knowledge held by the great masters in every discipline—from the spiritual to the mundane—is, collectively, appearance appearing in Consciousness.

Yet, Consciousness is not just a 'thing'. It has no colour, taste, form, sound, sensation, dimension, weight, or substance. It doesn't take up space, yet space appears in it. It doesn't depend on time, yet time is measured within it. It cannot be investigated or discovered or subjected to empirical method, yet it cannot be denied, for the very act of denying Consciousness demands Consciousness. It is the one Reality that cannot be grasped, yet is undeniable. It is Consciousness itself that puts every other possibility in doubt.

The Self and the Soul

The Self is changeless Consciousness. The Self is omnipresent. The Self is not a transmigrating soul. Most religious people have difficulty believing this, for no part of the Self comes down, goes up or flies off to another world in the afterlife. The Self is recognized as what it really is only when the veil of ignorance that covers it is removed. We change, but the Self never changes. It is we who carry the veil of ignorance that causes our suffering. Nothing happens to the Self. The individual soul has its being in the Self. This embodied soul is not the Self but it does exist as a body more subtle than the physical and visible body.

> *'All souls are intrinsically free from old age and death. But by imagining senility and death, and being engrossed in that thought, they deviate from their nature.'*
> —Gaudapada (8th century AD)

The individual soul is also a thought-form, a creation of the ego-mind arising from the false identification of the Self with its limiting adjuncts, i.e. the physical and subtle bodies. It is this false identification that gives rise to the sense or notion of an atomic soul, functioning either as the body-mind or as a finite spirit inhabiting the body. Yes, the individual soul does exist, but relatively speaking; no, it is not the Self, nor is it the physical body.

However, both the subtle and gross bodies are important as adjuncts of the Self and they function as vehicles through which all experiences occur. Neither the physical eye nor the mind has any power of vision, for the real Eye is the Self—formless, infinite and pure Consciousness.

The Self itself does not see forms, for forms are created by the very act of seeing. The Self is not a subject observing an object. It can only be Self-experienced, it can never be an object of thought or perception. This is why the ancient seers (*rishis*) described it as 'Not this. Not this.' The Self cannot be described, but like love, it must be directly felt. It is never seen, but it can be realized. Its true nature is bliss (*Ananda*).

Do you live within the house called the Self or is the house called the Self within you? The answer is both and neither. One must always remain steadfast, just like that place which is naturally always yours—the Self. To feel the Self within one's body is to experience pure light in a windless place. To feel the Self as all-pervading is to experience a vast and waveless ocean. There is no such thing as attainment, since the supreme Self is the ever-present and ever-attained single Whole. The Self—one's authentic true nature—is the substratum of all happiness in this and any other world. The locus of the Self is not in space or time; the locus is everywhere, nowhere and is always now.

The Self includes both ignorance and knowledge and at the same time, it transcends this polarity, just like it transcends all polarities. In the unmanifested state, the universe exists as pure potentiality (*Shakti*). This pure potentiality has its being in the Self. All that we perceive and do not perceive also has its being in the Self. Water remains what it is, with or without currents and waves. The Self is the same.

It is Consciousness, it is not 'consciousness-of-something'. Yet, 'consciousness-of-something' has its being in Consciousness, i.e. the Self. Whatever the appearance is, the Self is 'Not this. Not this'. It is so refined, it transcends essence. We do not and cannot understand this world except in terms of an appearance—an evanescent picture show. All we are ever truly witnessing is the Self, even though it is disguised by appearances. Therefore, there is nothing we can 'teach' about the Self, since only 'things' can be taught and the Self is not a thing. The Sages affirm that silence is the highest and truest teaching.

As is the case with Self, Consciousness is not perceived or known, yet it exists. It must exist in order for anything to be known. Knowledge is Consciousness itself. The Self is not a locus of perception; it is not the 'point of view' from which the world is seen. Rather, the Self is the Awareness of the locus, while it is the ego that identifies itself with the locus. The Self always remains what it is—Consciousness itself.

The Self is the source. It is indescribable. It is not dead, but the essence of life itself. It can never be born and it can never die. This is the basis of the *ajata* (non-creation) doctrine of Vedanta. The founding fathers of quantum physics understood this. They drew their inspiration from the Upanishads and the Bhagavad Gita. When all delusion is removed, what remains is the pristine Self. The Self is not known directly, but conceptually and empirically and remains a mystery. It is too intimate and immediate for us to see or understand. It is not a 'thing' we can observe or even grasp with the intellect.

Whatever we speak of the Self is the Self. There is nothing outside the Self that discusses or knows about it. There is nothing that is even opposite to the Self. Thus, the understanding of the Self is the Self. The Self can neither exist, nor can it not exist. What a wonder!

Direct experience is the only proof of the Self, but this proof is always private. It is known neither by inference, deduction, logic, science, philosophy, or scripture. Thus, even though the Self is ever-present, it remains a perpetual mystery to the calculative and empirical mind. Only a skilfully instructed inner experience will help in attaining full realization of the Self.

Ultimately, there is no non-self, only the Self. The false belief in the reality of a non-self, i.e. of 'otherness' is the illusion that disappears when the true nature of the Self is revealed through direct experience. The Self is inescapable. All experiences, including pure experience—meaning Self-awareness without an object—is included within it. The only way out of the hopeless and empty desert of the not-Self, i.e. the ego is to become conscious of what we already are—the Self.

Belief in the reality of a past and a future is what calls forth the illusion of reincarnation. In reality, there is no reincarnation of the undying Self. The Self, which is pure Knowledge, contains within itself both ignorance and ordinary knowledge. The Self manifests as this and that, and not as 'not-this' and 'not-that', yet It is always hidden from view. Although, the Self is Knowledge, it cannot be known by the mind or experienced by the senses.

The Self permeates the sense organs (eyes, ears, etc), but does not have its being in the organs; the organs, however, have their being in the Self. It is solely a mass of pure Consciousness; and it is of the nature of Bliss (*Ananda*).

The Self cannot be described, but like love, it can be experienced. And just like love not experienced, the Self not experienced is the greatest poverty. To experience the Self is to be the Self—no duality. Nothing could be more personal than the Self. It is pure intimacy, it is one's own. Paradoxically, it is the same 'one's own' as the 'one's own' of every other creature in every corner of creation.

Body and Mind

The real meaning of 'original sin' is the thought, 'I am this body.' It is all downhill from there until we start asking the question, 'Who am I?' Our physical life is very short; all the elements that make the man are now dissolving and falling apart. The brain acts as a delivery system, but the 'moment' of knowing belongs to Consciousness. The brain itself does not know. Brain waves continue through all the three states—waking, dreaming and deep sleep—only their patterns differ. For those whose God is empiricism, brain waves and feedback are the only true indications that Consciousness is present. For those who have realized the Self, however, Consciousness itself is the only true indication that Consciousness and by extension, 'substance' is present.

Substance has its being in Consciousness and never leaves it—beyond appearance, there is no duality. The concept of brain activity is a 'thought' which has Consciousness as its source. Brain and mind are two sides of the same coin—one side is tangible while the other is intangible, yet undeniable. The brain cannot know the Self directly, therefore, it is ignorant of the Self, except as a concept. The intangible Self is forever beyond the reach of the organ called the brain. Nevertheless, the brain has its being in Consciousness, just like everything else.

In reality, thoughts do not spring up in the brain, they spring up in Consciousness. Therefore, Consciousness is the source of thought. A thought is not the same thing as a brain activity. Without the light of Consciousness, body and brain would become inert, like a carcass or a rock. It is inconceivable that the gross brain is the source of the subtle Consciousness. It is paradoxical that unless the body is taken to be the Self, the world of moving and unmoving objects that demands an observing subject cannot be seen. Thus, those who know the true nature of the Self do not see the world in the same way as those who are ignorant of the Self and falsely identify it with the body. In other words, they they see the world in a radically different context.

Mind

The notions of mind, ego-self and a localized subject are superimposed on the substratum of Consciousness. Their reality is inferred, not proven. No one actually sees or touches the mind, ego or subjective self. What is easily overlooked is that these ephemeral notions actually shape and structure the very experience from which their existence is inferred. Thus, they become self-fulfilling prophecies that arise in the Consciousness. They sprout at the place where energy begins to manifest in pure Consciousness.

Mind is nothing more or less than a steady stream of thoughts passing over the substratum of pure Consciousness. Without the substratum, there is no mind, thought, ego, or subjective self. Mind alone will never be able to unravel the mystery of Creation. In order to arrive at the source, the mind must be turned aside from all else and towards the undying Self. The 'reactive mind', which is a foreign installation and not our true nature, sees change and transformation as threats to its survival, which is true. It rebels against any genuine spiritual practice we choose to embark upon.

Since the world-appearance is nothing but mind, the truth of it depends upon the truth of the mind, which puts us in a highly precarious position. The mind cannot be counted on; it is discontinuous and vanishes during sleep, swoon or a state of shock. It can easily delude and mislead us. Much of the content of mind is buried in the unconscious, thus influencing our behaviour unknowingly, and often, negatively. The mind is full of notions which are the progeny of primordial ignorance.

Like an ant or a bee, the mind has sufficient aptitude to be able to navigate and survive for a short span in a circumscribed environment. The mind is only thoughts—if there are no thoughts, there will be no mind, and if there is no mind, there will be no thoughts. Mind is the flow of appearances, both subtle and gross. When all appearances disappear, so does the mind. It is not a thing that can be found. It is a single category—the category of all appearances. Mind, identified with the world-appearance, is illusory and unreal. Identified with the Self, mind is real. But in itself, it is neither real nor unreal—it has a borrowed existence. Whatever is appearing is mind and it appears to change with changing appearances. Mind experiences what the senses, memory and intellect construct.

It is 'context', while appearance is 'content'—the two belong to each other. Conditioned and impure mind shapes content whereas unconditioned mind is pure.

The Self is realized with a pure mind—a mind emptied of all empirical, conceptual and buried content. Whatever a mirage represents has no existence other than being an idea in the mind. Mind is not mine. Where did it come from? Who am I? Mind is simply the conjunction of Consciousness and *prana* (vital force). Mind manifests as memories, names and forms, as well as qualities, such as colours, sounds, tastes and odours.

Mind is subtle; body is gross. Mind and body are not separate, not different—no body means no mind; no mind means no body.

The Self cannot be known by the mind; to know something implies a relationship. A pure mind has its being in the Self and is not separate. How can the absolute Self stand in relation to anything relative, such as a 'conditioned mind' or 'material body'? Nevertheless, mind and body have their being in the Self.

Conditioned mind is the phenomenon or appearance (revealed); it is not the noumenal 'thing-in-itself' (the hidden).

The appearance of a stone is not the hidden reality of the stone. Whether there truly is a hidden 'thing-in-itself' behind the stone's appearance is another question. Our failure to 'see' the hidden is a limitation of our bodily apparatus. Nevertheless, the true ground of both the revealed and the hidden is pure Consciousness—the Self. We are that Self, but we have not fully realized it.

All our images of the world share a common ground. However, our images are not that ground. Being self-ignorant, we don't know the ground; we can only infer a material ground from the images that appear. This relative ground should not be confused with the ultimate ground of pure Consciousness. Mind is whatever the organism throws up on the screen of Consciousness. Even the organism I call 'my body' is an appearance in Consciousness. Who am I?

Mind is the context of all experiences, including the illusory experience of subject/object duality, i.e. 'me' versus 'you', 'he', 'she', 'them' and 'it'. Mind with definitive (objective) content is the first manifestation of *Maya* (illusion); while subject-object duality is the second manifestation. In reality, both manifestations occur simultaneously. It is true that all recognition is based on memory. Inherent mental tendencies (*vasanas*) have their roots in memory, whether conscious or buried. When memory is erased, our self-created world and everything in it also disappears.

Past memory drives present action, producing future results, which in turn get stored in memory. In this way, the content of the memory bank is modified incrementally over time. This is the grand movie that each of us creates for ourselves, with or without a camera in hand. It is called *Maya* (illusion).

Memory shapes actions and actions create new memories. New memories modify the nature of future actions. In this way, our actions modify the organism, i.e. our body, incrementally. This modification of the body over time is called evolution. Evolution demands memory and memory demands Consciousness. Consciousness is the basis of everything and is untouched by evolution. Even if memory and the power of rational thought are utterly destroyed, intelligence remains.

We should never forget this when dealing with those who are intellectually handicapped. Treat them with respect. Treat all life forms, even the lowliest, with respect. The world manifested is called 'mind'; the world unmanifested is called 'Self'. Since the first has its being in the second, mind is also Self. Self, however, is never mind.

The Watcher and the Witness

Both the watcher and his object are mental creations. The Self is their substratum, yet it transcends both. When the watcher is, in truth, Consciousness itself, who is left to watch the watcher? How can you turn to see who you are when who you truly are is the witness of the watcher? The watcher is illusory and unreal—he is a thought-form, i.e. the ego-self. When the watcher awakens, he knows himself only as the witness—the pure Consciousness. Therefore, the watcher has his being in the witness. The phenomenon of recognition forces us to infer a witness, otherwise there is only blindness or non-experience. The question is, 'What is the nature of the witness and how can we discover it?' No matter how subtle or gross the object—a thought, feeling, rock or even our image in a mirror—there must be a witness to it. What is this witness? It is the Self, our true nature.

The Ego

The ego is an empty apparition.

> *'Shape without form, shade without colour, Paralyzed force, gesture without motion...'*
> —*The Hollow Men*, T.S. Eliot (1888–1965)

> *'Understand that when the ego dies and the real Self is realized as the One Reality, then there remains only that real Self, who is pure Consciousness.'*
> —Ramana Maharshi (1879–1950)

Who we are will always remain innocent, despite the ego-mind's ignorant efforts to prove otherwise. With the death of the ego, there is no more death. As for bodies, they come and go. The rigid true believer is just the ego whose nature is to hide or dominate or distort the truth. The ego-mind is aware of itself as conscious, yet this ordinary consciousness is a weak and distorted revelation of the light of pure Consciousness, and the ego-mind's intelligence is merely a reflected intelligence borrowed from the Self.

Men are afraid to lose the ego because they believe the ego to be themselves and they fear that with the death of the ego, they shall cease to be. Nothing could be further from the truth. The ego is merely a thought-form that has no real existence. As long as we believe that our ego is something real, we will be stuck with it. Once we are convinced that the ego is unreal, we will be able to let it go, just as a man is no longer afraid of his shadow once he realizes that it is unreal and has no power to harm him.

The lure of the ego-mind draws us away from our true purpose. The seed of a noxious weed can be extinguished by refusing to give it moisture, earth and light. So, it is when we refuse to feed and pamper the ego, that it finally goes.

The ego exists as a function of the power of Consciousness and creates 'names and forms', i.e. things. Although the ego is not different from Being-Consciousness, it is nevertheless *Maya* (illusion). The ego is unreal; it is a false assumption.

Solipsism, which is the view that the small, limited self is all that can be known to exist, still demands a subject (the ego) and its objects. The solipsist falsely lives in a self-created prison. The true Self, however, demands neither subject nor object and knows no boundaries.

Just as there is a material reality that will cause problems if misperceived, the Self too—wrongly identified with the ego—will be falsely accused for our suffering. The ego is not the Self, but rather a delusion of the mind that keeps us separate, confused and in pain. Just how we do not blame the moon when its light is blocked by dense clouds, we should not blame the Self when our natural happiness is covered by our dense ignorance.

There is no original sin, only original ignorance. There is no divine punishment, only self-created suffering born out of self-ignorance. The choice to awaken is ours and ours alone. The egoic mind is an oppressor, and until it is conquered, there will be no justice and peace in this world. It is only the ego-mind that is monitoring the ego-mind. That is how bad it is for humanity!

We cannot remove ignorance with ignorance, or darkness with darkness. Just as darkness demands light in order to disappear, the ego—which is ignorance—must be exposed and relinquished by the light of Knowledge of the Self. And all of this has nothing to do with intellectual prowess—nothing at all. It has everything to do with self-effort and Grace.

The ego is unreal; it is a creation of the mind. The mind is its own grindstone, it polishes the ego. Do not speak to the ego, one's own or another's. It will only get bigger, stronger and more dishonest. Speak to the Self. It is the misperceiving of the true nature of the Self—a misperception which is called 'the ego-self'—that is the cause of suffering, violence, stress, anxiety and the premature weakening of the body.

The waking state is itself a dream. The ego-'I' is both the main character of this dream as well as its creator. The ego's quest for the Self is also the main theme of this dream. The search is contained in the dream, and the dream is unreal. Hence, the adage of the Sage Ramana Maharshi, 'You are already that which you seek.' We need to only awaken from this waking state of dream. If there is no real small 'I', if the ego is a complete fabrication, then who reincarnates? It cannot be the Self or the present body, so then, who? The ego-mind's attachment to the idea of an earlier life and an afterlife is its own creation.

The philosopher Jean-Paul Sartre believed that the ego is determined and not free. The Vedantic Sages hold that the ego is an illusion; a mistaken identification of the mind with the Self. They both agree that the ego is not free. As long as one feels separate, one must assume personal responsibility for one's loneliness and isolation. When the sense of 'doership' disappears, so does the ego, and along with it, the egoic sense of responsibility. Very few can understand this. Even fewer can let go of the false egoic sense of responsibility and yet remain responsible. War is the disease of the ego—all forms of war.

Memory

All recognition is based on memory; destroy memory and the world we think we know disappears. The urge to recreate remembered pleasures in the future clouds the tranquility and expansiveness of the eternal present.

Intellect

The universe is a fluid and dynamic architecture which is the living creation of a supreme, yet unfathomable Creator. The intellect can stand in awe of its own source but will never grasp it. The Self permeates its own effect which is the intellect.

The intellect, which makes distinctions and apprehends objects, cannot function in the absence of distinctions and objects. Thus, in any objectless state such as deep sleep or the pure Awareness of deep meditation, the intellect rests in silence.

Linear minds that think solely in terms of specific results—specific environments, specific actions, specific sequences, specific timeline—never quite arrive at the specific goal. There is always an aura of disappointment and incompleteness. Wholeness is a space to come from, not a place to arrive at.

Intellectuals who have not directly known the silent objectless state of deep meditation cannot conceive that in the absence of all objects and distinctions, anything other than an unconscious state is possible. Many believe, therefore, that Consciousness is always 'consciousness-of-something'. Nothing could be further from the truth.

When advanced meditators speak about their experience of the objectless state, the strict empiricists are highly sceptical. Those with a scientific bent say that there is no evidence to support the claims of the mystics. Of course there is no evidence. Evidence always demands an object and what the meditators speak of is unbounded and objectless. The body is not apart from the Self. It is our mental modifications which create the false impression of a separate body and a separate Self.

The individual time-traveling eternal soul is a false creation of the ego-intellect. It is as ephemeral and relative as the physical body it inhabits. It is the intellect which while meditating repeats the *mantra*, but this silent repetition gradually fades away and merges into silent Awareness (*samadhi*).

Faith is a leap, a mode of the intellect and emotions; not Grace, which is a bestowal. Abstract space is purely intellectual, whereas real space is substance, albeit an extremely subtle substance (ether, *akasha*). The intellect is subject to *Maya* (illusion) and is therefore limited. The intellect cannot reach to Reality. It is the delusions of the intellect which keep us in a hellish, earthbound condition. The intellectual process in itself involves vital energy (*prana*), which in turn is not different from Consciousness. The 'I'-thought, which is a function of the intellect, arises from the Heart, which is the seat of the intellect. This 'I'-thought is the core thought, i.e. the ego; it is not the true Self.

A thought or a concept can only truly represent itself and not the thing it refers to. A thought cannot embrace itself; it is singular. The aspirant attains the Self through seeking, not by scholarship and intellectual analysis. Conceptual knowledge can only serve as a guidepost. All thoughts of insentient matter, observation (from microscopic to macrocosmic), theory, and evidence demands Consciousness. We can never get outside of Consciousness in order to verify the existence of the non-conscious. We may infer it, but we cannot prove it. The moment we define or identify ourselves, we limit ourselves to something we are not. This is ignorance.

Triads and Opposites

The triads (related groups of three such as 'perceiver, perceiving, perceived', 'knower, knowing, known', 'doer, doing, done' etc.) arise as a function of the ego-sense; and it arises the pairs of opposites ('ignorance, knowledge', 'right, wrong' etc.). If the seeker enters the Heart through self-enquiry and realizes the Self, all the triads and pairs of opposites will no longer appear real. They will be obliterated, forever.

Sleeping and Dreaming

It is a truism that while a man is dreaming, he does not know he is in a dream; he only knows upon awakening. Likewise, our waking state is a dream but we are not aware in the waking state. Only when we awaken from the waking state do we know that we were dreaming. Deep sleep is a mass of Consciousness covered by a blanket of ignorance. Consciousness is reality and ignorance is the absence thereof. Illusion and delusion are born of ignorance and ultimately are sublated* by Knowledge, i.e. pure Consciousness.

The Sage may close his eyes and appear to sleep, but he remains awake within. Self-awareness persists in sleep, even though all mental activity is in complete suspension. Deep sleep, dreaming and ordinary waking states are simply thin blankets that temporarily cover the underlying ocean of Self-awareness. You can live a good dream, you can live a bad dream, you can live a new dream, but the whole point is to 'awaken' from the dream.

Death and Immortality

'A free man thinks of nothing less than of death; and his wisdom is a meditation not of death, but of life.'
—Baruch Spinoza (1632–1677)

The moment we are born, we are dying—'the body', that is. When we consider the many unpleasant ways there are to die, it makes more sense to pierce the illusion of dying rather than waste time planning our funeral. The subtle body departs with the death of the gross body—it does not die. This subtle body is not the Self. 'Gross body', 'subtle body'—these are relative things. The Self is Absolute.

Death is not a journey, it is a transformation. No one goes anywhere. There is only one Consciousness, one intelligence and we are it. We must open our eyes. Deathlessness is attained through surrender, not Yoga. Yoga is action for purification, but purification precedes surrender.

---

*'sublate' (def.): to negate yet preserve as a potential possibility; assimilate (a smaller entity) into a larger one.

Who knows what happens after the dissolution of our human form? Does consciousness of 'otherness' continue after death? Does awareness resolve itself into a silent beingness which is void of all objectivity? We will see it when it happens. Or, we won't.

The terrible fear of complete extinction at the time of death is merely a frightening thought. In truth, extinction is impossible to conceive or experience. Consciousness is not a 'thing' that can be exterminated, obliterated or destroyed. This is our immortality.

2

BEING
What Is Being?

'Being is. Being is in-itself. Being is what it is.'
—Jean-Paul Sartre (1905–1980)

'Man is the neighbour of Being.'
—Martin Heidegger (1889–1976)

Being is the primal state of love in which there is no 'otherness' to fear. Ultimately, there is no separateness, no duality. We must erase the dualistic programming that destroys our sanity and equilibrium, and return to our Original State. Our programmes are contained in subconscious mental files and the totality of these files is called 'conditioned mind'. We think of this mind as ours, but it is installed from our environment and our ancestors.

When a file is opened, mind becomes activated and then the trouble starts. We must delete these files. In the Original State, all programmes have been deleted, leaving only our natural mind. Being-Consciousness itself remains as it has always been—untouched, pure, limitless and undivided. The only absolute certitude we have is the certitude of Being—i.e. the certitude, 'I am'. This 'I am' has no adjective attached, and therefore, it is not the deluding ego. This 'I am', standing alone, is the only 'fact' that is direct, immediate and incontrovertible. It is the foundation of everything. Being persists through all the apparent states of consciousness—waking, dreaming and sleeping.

Man is not tied or bound to Being, rather man is not separate from Being. There is neither imprisonment nor the duality of separation. Man is the intimate lover who never leaves Being. What remains is Self-luminous Being-Consciousness (*Sat-Chit*). All else is a fairy tale—unreal.

The Being of the world is hidden, It is what it is; however, the Being of the world-appearance is Consciousness. Even so, the hidden also has its being in Consciousness. Form and movement have no Being in themselves, they are neither real nor unreal, yet in order for them to appear, there must be Being. All apparent differences in the phenomenal world are finally resolved in the unified field of Being.

The Supreme Being (*Brahman*)

'Being is not God.'
—Martin Heidegger (1889–1976)

Nevertheless, God (*Shiva*) has His being in Being. He is *saguna* (the Absolute with qualities). This entire cosmos is under the control of a Supreme Intelligence and there is nothing which operates independently. From the microscopic to the macrocosmic, the universe is clearly a manifestation of the Supreme Intelligence.

Suffering arises from the illusion of a separate, individuated self or soul who makes choices freely and independently of the Supreme power. If we believe that we are finite creatures who have ultimate free will, we must assume freedom of choice. In fact, we have no other option. Clearly, an individuated, intelligent entity, both logically and by extension, must be making its own choices. This false but seemingly necessary illusion, however, adds to our suffering as it is the inevitable extension of the myth of a separate individuated existence. The alternative option to this condition of pain is to consciously make a choice in favour of a single, Supreme force that creates, permeates and controls the entire cosmos as the power of Consciousness and Grace.

> *'If you think, "I have known Brahman (the impersonal absolute reality) well enough", then you have known only the very little expression that It has among the gods. Therefore, Brahman is still to be deliberated on...'*
>
> —Kena Upanishad

God, Gods and celestials have their being in Being (*Brahman*). The World appears within the Supreme Being, stays in it and gets resolved into it. No effort is involved. Power (*Shakti*) takes care of everything. The dissolution of the universe is not the extinction of the universe, just like deep sleep is not the extinction of Consciousness. Their appearance and disappearance are pulsations (*Shakti*), emanating from the Supreme Being. There is something that generates the primal impulse and this something is the *Shakti* inherent in the Supreme Being. Whatever we do in service or in contribution is an offering to the Supreme Being. This is the true meaning of renunciation. It is not a set of rules or a particular behaviour or an artificial self-denial.

The laws of cause and effect, space and time, name and form, apply to the content of appearances and not to the noumenal (hidden) ground of the 'in-itself'. The ground of the 'in-itself' is nothing more than the interplay of energies which themselves arise from the pure potentiality of the *Shakti* inherent in the Supreme Being. Limitless power is both transcendent and immanent within the indivisible, non-dual reality—the 'One without a Second.'

The Supreme Being manifests creative intelligence. From

the subtle to the gross, creative intelligence first manifests as etheric space (*akasha*), then energy, substance, form and name. Being-Consciousness contains within itself all possibilities. The Power inherent in the Supreme Intelligence manifests as qualities (colours, sounds, sensations, shapes etc.). If this infinite Power was to withdraw into pure potentiality, then all the qualities, along with the powers of seeing, hearing, feeling and thinking, would withdraw into the void.

Not inert like a rock, but changeable like the form of a snake, the Supreme Being can assume any form. It is simultaneously unmoving and dynamic—transcendent and immanent. Man as Consciousness is not different from the Supreme Being as Consciousness—there is no duality. The Supreme Being is pure intelligence; the mind, brain, memory and intellect is its creation.

The Supreme Being cannot be compared to an artist or a builder—it doesn't 'do' art or 'do' building. The Supreme Being, manifesting as God (*Shiva*), doesn't function in any linear sense. God is both immanent and transcendent and therefore everything is always happening (or not) now. It is the limited, time-bound mind that conceives a specific series of events occurring within a specific environment producing specific results. In reality, there is no such thing, and there are no specific series, no specific events, no specific results.

The creative intelligence of the Supreme Being is spontaneous, natural and effortless; it is absolutely coherent, and what appears to be incoherent is always sublated by a larger coherence. This ultimate coherence is like the finest music and sweetest bliss. The Supreme Being cannot be defined, grasped or appreciated by the calculative and acquisitive mind.

Things do not exist in relation to the Supreme Being, only in relation to other things. To one for whom things exist, the Supreme Being does not exist and to one for whom the Supreme Being exists, things do not exist. For the Sage, who appears to walk around and speak with others, his body does not exist.

Still, he eats and washes himself like any ordinary human being. This is a paradox that only the Sage understands.

The Sage, being perfectly surrendered to the Supreme Being, also functions with a creative intelligence that is spontaneous, natural and effortless. Every organic being is an eye of the Supreme Intelligence. The infinite collectivity of both organic and celestial beings must be the infinite eye of that intelligence.

God

> *'Philosophy decides neither for nor against the existence of God. It remains indifferent.'*
> —Martin Heidegger (1889–1976)

> *'Shiva is the Being assuming all forms and the Consciousness seeing them. That is to say, Shiva is the background underlying both the subject and the object. Everything has its being in Shiva and because of Shiva.'*
> —Ramana Maharshi (1879–1950)

God (*Shiva*) has no attributes. If He had attributes, He would be in relativity and therefore not real. We call God He, but in reality, God is neither a He nor a She and definitely not an It. As long as we believe we are separate, we believe we have free will. In order to function, we must assume this. When we awaken, we realize that 'All is God's doing.' The real nature of God is hidden within His manifestations. If we turn something sacred into an object, it is no longer sacred. Alternatively, we can use an object to symbolize the sacred for the purpose of meditation and worship.

God is neither more nor less than the beginningless, immeasurable power of Consciousness. This power is at the basis of everything, including the dualistic polarities that we call knowledge and ignorance, good and evil, etc. God is the intelligent source of the original creative impulse. God includes both the manifest and the unmanifest—there is no inherent contradiction.

God is neither an objective nor a subjective reality: God is the reality that includes everything.

God (*Shiva*) cannot truly be an object of thought because the thinker is not independent of God; in short, the subject cannot become its own object, and the object cannot become its own subject. All duality is relative and, ultimately, unreal. The real is 'One without a second'. God is the cosmic mass of pure Consciousness; that is to say, God is not different from Being. God is Being; and Being is alive, not inert or abstract. We are not different from this ocean of Being as God (*Shiva*); all there is, has ever been, or will ever be is Being.

God is that, whatever it may be, from which we come. God is the ultimate source. Trying to grasp the source with our mind would be comparable to Michelangelo's sculpture 'Adonis' attempting to understand its creator, Michelangelo. Impossible!

God, as something interior or exterior, is dead. But God as Being is everything, everywhere, and in fact, is life itself. Only in our ignorance do we think of God as separate. To know God is to be one with God. There is no duality.

The Absolute

> *'Quantum theory...reveals a basic oneness of the Universe. It shows that we cannot decompose the world into independently existing smallest units. As we penetrate into matter, nature does not show us any isolated 'basic building blocks', but rather appears as a complicated web of relations between the various parts of the whole.'*
> —Fritjof Capra (1939–present)

The universal flow arising within the absolute remains within the absolute. It has nowhere else to go. Nothing leaves the absolute; nothing enters it. The Absolute is nowhere except 'Here' and at no time except 'Now'.

Existence

The direct experience of our own existence shines as the mystic silence and is the true Self behind the fictitious first person, 'I'. There is 'existence', i.e. pure Consciousness, and there is 'existence', i.e. name and form. 'The 'existence', with its apparent multiple manifestations, is sublated by 'Existence'.

An object known is identical with a known object. It is a tautology. When there is no object, there is nothing to be known and there is no object until it is known. Whatever the object known is, it exists; it exists as a known object within Existence itself. Beyond the appearance, there is no such thing as a distinct, discrete object—all is one. Existence exists before any particularized manifestation.

Out of pure Existence, space manifests as the extremely subtle ether (*akasha*), and then comes the rest. We cannot enquire about that which does not exist. Something exists for us when it is known. We can only enquire about that which is either known to exist or postulated to exist. In the latter instance, it is the postulation itself that exists, not what is being postulated.

Enquiry can also begin with a 'clue' that something exists. What we know or postulate about becomes a part of our description of the world, and this description, although as necessary as a road map to a traveller, is not reality. Whatever 'exists' has its being in 'Existence' itself; nothing else exists beyond Existence. Existence cannot come into being from non-existence, just as 'something' cannot emerge from 'nothing'. Existence must be beginningless and cannot itself be caused. So, what then is the primal cause of causality? Nothing. There is no primal cause. Causality, like time and road maps, is an invention of the mind.

Consciousness of an existent thing corresponds only to qualities, i.e. colours, sounds, sensations, tastes, odours and forms—the thing 'in-itself' is not known. If we say the Absolute exists, then in relationship to what? Something always exists in relation to something else. By definition, nothing stands apart from the Absolute; therefore, the Absolute cannot be said to exist. If we say that the Absolute exists, then there must necessarily be something that does not exist; otherwise the term 'exist' is meaningless. If we say that something is 'hot', then there must be something that is 'cold'. If everything is 'hot', then the term 'hot' becomes meaningless, since 'hot' demands its opposite, 'cold', in order to be 'hot'.

If we say the Absolute does not exist, then in relation to what does it not exist? Thus, the Absolute cannot be said to not exist. If we say the Absolute is 'all' that exists, then again, in relation to what? Without 'non-existence', the term 'existence' becomes meaningless, and vice versa. Thus, the Absolute must transcend both existence and non-existence.

The noumenal world, i.e. the world which is hidden from direct experience is inherent in the Absolute and is neither separate nor independent. Therefore, it neither exists nor does it not exist. The same is true of the phenomenal world which is an appearance that is revealed but which by definition cannot reveal the noumenal. The phenomenal, too, is inherent in the Absolute and is therefore neither separate nor independent. Thus, as with the noumenal, the phenomenal neither exists nor does it not exist.

Whatever appears as separate and distinct is 'not', except as an appearance. Neither does existence nor non-existence exist; neither do they not exist. The Self is, yet it transcends the relativities of existence and non-existence. Reality is beyond all the pairs of opposites created by the polar mind.

Infinity

That which is finite has no relationship to that which is infinite, yet the measurable, relative finite exists within the immeasurable, absolute infinite. The view that the finite is somehow distinct from the infinite and thus distinct from other finites is a delusion.

Similar to the phenomenon of a mirage, the notion of distinct finites is a false appearance, an unreal creation of the mind. There is no duality in reality.

The Source

What does evolution lead to? All evolution leads back to the source. You are already that which you seek, so stop seeking. You are already that which you are becoming, so stop becoming. Nothing ever leaves the source.

Source always remains what it is—'Source'. As long as we feel disconnected from our true Source—something which is impossible—we feel isolated and alone in the universe.

The Void

> *'Realize the Self always to be neither above nor below, nor on either side, nor without nor within, but to be eternal and shining beyond the sublime Void.'*
> —*Atma Sakshatkara*, The Agamas

The void is not a state of non-Being; emptiness is not nothingness. Void is the extremely subtle space of pure, infinite potentiality (*akasha*).

3

THE HUMAN CONDITION

*'On Margate Sands. I can connect
Nothing with nothing.'*
—*The Wasteland*, T.S. Eliot (1888–1965)

Suffering and Negativity

'Unrelieved stress is the cause of all disease.'
—Dr Hans Selye (1907-1982)

We can never escape Consciousness, thus exists the futility of suicide. Clearing repressed, negative 'junk' from the unconscious is essential, since what is buried in our internal delusional 'mud', forms a major part of the screen or filter through which we perceive our world, as well as ourselves.

Until we become conscious of our unconscious, negative, behavioural patterns and clear them, they will be recycled by the mind repetitively and endlessly. We will be the cousins of hamsters in a cage, continuously running on a wheel that leads to nowhere other than complete exhaustion and death.

Others can see our unconscious patterns long before we do, and they silently mock us. Negative patterns and addictions thrive in the unconscious, where our doubts and fears become a self-fulfilling prophecy. Self-enquiry, meditation and conscious breathing (*pranayama*) are powerful allies for driving away these life-destroying demons.

Projection

'Projection' is the past experience of the mind overlaid on the data of the present, creating misperception or illusion, and producing wrong or inappropriate actions. Our world is familiar to us because of past experiences, and the way we see this world is determined by those experiences. We unconsciously project past experiences on the present situation, thus, we never see clearly what is before us, as it actually is.

The mind projects the resentment building up inside onto other people and situations, turning its wrath upon them. This is called revenge. Very often, it is the innocent who suffer. It is easier and more comfortable to focus on the faults of others than to assume responsibility for our own failings and delusions.

Self-talk

The bulk of our self-talk is an inner dialogue that is rooted in fear and resentment, and is the source of our ambivalence, apathy and frustration in life. Our negative self-talk gets transmitted into our environment, like a virus, infecting our listeners and triggering their insecurities. Shut off the internal dialogue, empty the mind and be free!

The Addiction of Approval

We feel compelled to seek and hold onto the approval of others, and this compulsion breeds resentment and ambivalence. We avoid the disapproval of others and thus we become inauthentic and conformist. If we have been subjected to much disapproval in our early years, we become timid, withdrawn and afraid to step forward; we become unable to function freely in the field of action. We must go beyond our addiction to approval and our fear of disapproval.

Denial and Suppression

The more we resist whatever it is we are unhappy with, the bigger the problem becomes. What we resist always persists, whereas the suppressed emotional pain that we allow ourselves to accept, feel and relinquish, disappears. Repression and denial are key factors in psychosomatically induced illnesses and aberrant, anti-social behaviour.

Practice moderation, but neither suppression nor denial. Dispassion is not denial. Denial is desire suppressed. Desire disappears and drowns in the ocean of fulfillment. Desirelessness is the state of the enlightened. For those seekers who are still in the dream of duality and experience the torment of insatiable desire, this desire must be channelled toward productivity, contribution and creativity. This does not mean self-denial. Self-denial leads to apathy in those who are ignorant of the Self.

Suppressed emotions add mass to unconscious and negative beliefs. Conscious breathing (*pranayama*) can thin out this emotional mass, making it easier to identify and transform the underlying destructive thought-forms.

Fear and Anxiety

> 'In this last of meeting places
> We grope together
> And avoid speech
> Gathered on this beach of the tumid river.'
> —*The Hollow Men*, T.S. Eliot (1888–1965)

> *'...believe that life is worth living and your belief will help create the fact.'*
>
> —William James (1842–1910)

Fear of the unknown is the driving force behind our resistance to change. Change has a ripple effect and one major event in our life can alter all our relationships and circumstances. Again, we can be faced with the unknown. We are always faced with the unknown.

Fear of loss of agreement, i.e. disapproval, rejection and so forth, pervades the collective consciousness, while the need to belong—sometimes at any cost—is a dominant primal drive.

We are controlled by our environment because fear of loss of agreement ties directly into the most primeval need of all—the need to survive. Only the Sage is completely free of this demon.

The 'I', which is the mind-created ego, cannot see the Self. However, the 'I' can merge with or lose itself in the Self. This is the destruction of the ego; this is freedom and the end of anxiety. Agitation is the source of illness, aggression and depression. We are not aware of our fundamental indestructibility and are therefore afraid. Thus, we cling to our various manifestations, most particularly our bodies and our unexamined assumptions. Forgetfulness of the Self creates anxiety and the tormenting sense of loneliness and isolation.

If we feel we are in the world, there will be fear. If we feel the world is in us, there will be no fear. The illusion that time is real creates fear of the future and attachment to the past, thus leading to individual and global anxiety. Anxiety is the falsely based emotion underlying violence and war. Let go of the future and the past, and 'Be Here Now'.

> *'It is from a second entity that fear comes.'*
> —Brihadaranyaka Upanishad

Fear is rooted in desire, attachment and the illusion of 'otherness'.

Our fear of the fears of others is what either paralyzes us or feeds our aggression. Despair is an intense form of fear and it is the driving force behind committing suicide. Only knowledge of the Self, i.e. direct Knowledge, releases us from all fears. Bliss is the fear-free state. Bliss is the Self. Fear is what underlies anger, grief, judgements, addictions, cruelty, dishonesty, stealing, violence, insanity and every kind of vice.

Fear breeds attachment; attachment breeds fear. Fear negates love; love negates fear. We lose our mind to wealth only because of our fear of poverty. Fear and passivity do not serve the unenlightened. The path of liberation demands courage and engagement. He who knows himself as the Self knows no fear. This is the great liberation. The attitude that 'All is God's doing' destroys fear.

Guilt

Personal guilt—conscious or unconscious, real or unreal—is the basis of self-sabotage, as well as self-destructive behaviour. Guilt, shame and self-hatred is the underlying pathology that perpetuates humanity's long history of atrocities. Projecting guilt is the ultimate weapon for justifying control and domination of others. When we know ourselves as guiltless, we allow others to be free.

Genocide is a projection of our personal guilt and self-hatred combined with the personal guilt and self-hatred of others, onto a collective 'them' determined by race, colour, creed, etc. It is a madness that first infects a single mind, and then spreads like a plague, ending with mass murder and destruction.

Guilt, shame and hatred, etc. are thought-forms pulsating deep within our psyche that—like all thought-forms—are mental creations superimposed upon the pure Self, much like a movie projected on a screen.

Jealousy and Competition

Undeniably, struggle and competition have been the hallmark of human history and show no signs of abating in the foreseeable future. We perceive the other as a threat or competitor and seek to defend against, control or dominate him. As the philosopher Jean-Paul Sartre famously stated, 'L'enfer, c'est les autres' (Hell is the others).

Jealousy and envy have their being in low self-esteem, arising from negative decisions we have made about ourselves, aided and abetted by others. Ignorance of our true nature, the Self, is the source of the problem. Self-knowledge is the only way out. Jealousy arises from comparison. Comparison generates desire. Desire thwarted creates more comparison. More comparison generates more jealousy. It is a vicious circle.

Suppressing desire and jealousy merely creates apathy and repressed rage. Ignorance causes this dilemma. Dwelling and focusing on another's apparent pleasure, happiness or success can also give rise to the feeling of personal deprivation, giving rise to jealousy and resentment. This often leads to covert or overt violence. Direct knowledge of the Self cancels out both jealousy and competition. Then, there is neither comparison nor apathy or rage.

Struggle

Why do human beings struggle with the world? Animals simply follow nature, day by day, minute by minute. They have no 'big' plans. They could teach us much if we had a little humility. Striving is born of an illusion—the illusion of separateness. What drives the will is an unconscious urge to return to wholeness, to return to the source. But this entire dynamic is absurd in the end, since the Self by its very nature never separates itself from the source. Self and source are, in fact, an identity.

When the reality that there is no separateness, no independent free will and no autonomous individual self finally dawns, all yearning and striving dissolve like shadows and mists before the morning Sun. Life is not useless or a waste, it is a *lila* (sportive play)—the play of *Shakti* (Power).

Our unconsciousness of the power inherent in Consciousness is what keeps us weak, poor and at war. We are that very power, but we forgot. We struggle in order to experience a moment of pleasure or relief, and then we go back to being unconscious. After that, we regain a little consciousness in order to struggle again for another brief experience of pleasure or relief. This is the 'History of the Human Race' in two sentences. The mind, being impermanent, cannot give us permanent pleasure or relief. Only the Self is eternal happiness and peace. We must become established in the Self, as the Self.

The Victim

A victim is a victim because he believes he is a victim and he will remain a victim until he abandons that belief. Our only way to freedom is to assume responsibility. When we do this, the victim inside us disappears.

The belief 'poor me' keeps us in a mindset that blocks our capacity to create what we want. We sell-out when we sacrifice something we cherish deeply, such as our freedom, integrity, autonomy or self-expression, for perceived survival needs.

Selling-out occurs when we sacrifice what we most love as a calling or mission for some other form of work that will merely pay our bills and take care of our physical survival. Sometimes we do what we don't love as a stepping stone to reach a position where we can do what we love. It is good, it is a test of our commitment and tenacity. Selling-out is the antithesis of courage and we despise ourselves for letting our fears make cowards of ourselves. 'Laziness' is another word for resignation—don't quit!

Addictions

We become addicted because we feel that something is missing or that we have been abandoned or abused. Our addiction temporarily fills the gap. When we finally realize that we are whole and complete in ourselves, there is no more hankering, and no more addiction. Whatever path we follow, we should stick to it with tenacity. That is the doorway to freedom. Letting go of addictions and awakening to the Self will occur concurrently.

Polarity

> *'Qualities are the pairs of opposites; turn away from them and the highest realization results.'*
> —*Devikalottara*, the Agamas

In a polar universe, one pole cannot exist without its opposite. The emotional and mental turbulence generated by the pairs of opposites, i.e. win-lose, hot-cold, good-bad, birth-death, etc. accelerates the decline of our body and destroys our health. Therefore, we must step out of polarity and realize the unbounded singularity of the Self. When we awaken to the Self, we become detached from the polarities. We simply witness them and are no longer enchanted, frightened or disturbed.

Preexisting Mental Tendencies (*Vasanas*)

It is the body that is involved in time, not the Self. Preexisting tendencies (*vasanas*) belong to the body and its soulmate, the mind. It is more important to destroy our compelling mental tendencies than to worry about our retirement plan. Retirement plans do not stop death whereas *vasanas* keep the wheel of suffering spinning, lifetime after lifetime.

Preexisting mental tendencies manifest as desires and aversions. According to the nature of their desires and aversions, life forms impinge on one another. All life forms feed off the energy, of the Sun, and then, of each other.

The already established *vasanas* within the body-mind begin to manifest due to the light of Consciousness. If these tendencies are vicious then the manifestation will be vicious, even though the light of Consciousness is itself without tendencies. Consciousness provides the intelligence and the vitality, not the tendency. Ignorance of the Self provides the tendency, and hence, the suffering.

4

ENLIGHTENMENT

Ignorance

'Carefully distinguishing the transcendental from the commonplace, the subtle from the gross, the Self must always be investigated into and realized by the vigilant.'
—*Atma Sakshatkara*, the Agamas

All ignorance is personal. When we perceive and react to the personal ignorance of another, that too becomes our personal ignorance. The personal 'other' does not exist outside of the Self, it is a false superimposition—a mirage. Ignorance of the Self is beginningless. There are two billion Christians, most of whom are ignorant of the Self; there are one and a half billion Muslims, most of whom are ignorant of the Self; there are one billion Hindus, most of whom are ignorant of the Self; there are half a billion Buddhists, most of whom are ignorant of the Self; there are a large numbers of atheists, most of whom are ignorant of the Self; there are a large numbers of materialists, all of whom are ignorant of the Self; and then there is the rest of us, most of whom are ignorant of the Self. It has always been like this.

The Self, realized, is the feeling that absolutely nothing is missing. All mental illness is born of ignorance; it is the delusive, vitiating feeling that something is wrong, something is missing or something is other than it actually is. All forms of ignorance are unreal. Ignorance is the absence of reality. There is no such thing as 'real' ignorance; rather, ignorance is a pure negation, a non-existence.

Our ignorance is not seen until it is removed. The mistake of misperceiving a rope as a snake resides in the intellect, which resides in the organism. So, we see a snake, which is unreal and think it to be real. Ignorance is always unreal. Ignorance is more than a mistaken thought or assumption; it is the falseness underlying the way we think and perceive. It is a delusion.

Suffering is the result of ignorance and is a false superimposition. The Self-realized cannot suffer, although their bodies may feel pain, like Jesus on the cross. Ignorance of the Self is beginningless, but not endless. Our ignorance of our true nature gives us the feeling of incompleteness.

Ignorance cannot be destroyed by attacking it. To do so is as ineffectual as Don Quixote tilting his lance and charging a windmill. The wise do not delude the ignorant. To do so is cruel.

Self-enquiry ('Who Am I?')

'This proposition "I am", "I exist", whenever I utter it or conceive it in my mind is necessarily true.'
—René Descartes (1596–1650)

The true identity of the 'I am' is the Absolute—the same Absolute that is the true identity of the 'I am' of every person, animal, plant and insect with which we share this planet. Consciousness only 'appears' to be localized and individualized as John, Mary, the cat, the dog, etc. In reality, it is simply one, reflected through many prisms called organisms. Consciousness itself is identical with that pure intelligence which is the ultimate source of this universe. Understanding and accepting this principle intellectually is the first step, but this alone will not take us beyond our illusion of separateness. It must be realized directly through meditation and self-enquiry in order for it to become our own discovery. It must be experienced.

We are already the Self, all we need do is let go of the idea that we are something other. There is no higher power that can save us, for in reality, we are that very higher power we seek and are fully capable of our own salvation. To fully awaken to the truth of the 'I am' as Consciousness is to awaken from the dream of separateness and to put an end to conflict. How can the Self be in conflict with the Self? Without division, there is no possibility of a fight. To realize that this vast and extraordinary universe is a unified field of Being and that 'I am' is also that Being is the great liberation.

Anyone who undertakes to awaken and heal himself through self-enquiry, meditation and conscious breathing (*pranayama*), will begin to feel or hear those deeper impulses which will give him direction in life. Those impulses will lead him to men and women of Knowledge. The ultimate delusion is the thought, 'I am this body'. The 'I am' is the single common factor of every thought we have, from the moment of our birth to the moment of our death.

Knowing the true nature of the 'I am' is infinitely more important than understanding quantum physics or the current market value of a barrel of oil. Through persistent self-enquiry, negative and entropic thinking will simply disappear from our internal screen. Our unexamined assumptions must be called into question relentlessly. The deepest question of all, 'Who or what or why am I?' pushes us to press through our unconsciousness and examine our own conditioning honestly.

Self-enquiry, meditation and conscious breathing (*pranayama*) are the most effective means for healing the mind of its negative tendencies. We are not contained by what is outside; rather, what appears to be outside is contained within us.

I think myself not to be, and still 'I am'. There is no escape. I am neither the subject nor the object, thus, there is no duality. I am the undying Self. I am no-'thing'; I am neither subtle nor gross.

When the 'I'-thought departs, so does the world. It is the egoic 'I'-thought that throws us into confusion and mixes us with the world. Until we awaken to who we really are, the beginningless 'I'-thought persists. The pure Consciousness of Being is Consciousness without an 'I'-thought or any other thought. The 'I'-thought, i.e. the notion of a finite, discrete self, is a delusion of the mind—it is the false ego.

The notion of 'thing-ness' is an illusion, one which includes that 'thing' called the universe. This notion creates a false duality and belongs to the 'I'-thought. Whatever the universe may be, it is not a 'thing'. The question, 'Who am I?' can be only partially answered by the intellect. To fully grasp the answer, the 'I am' in its true nature must be directly experienced. Those dominated by desires will be driven to actions, whereas those with few desires and who seek Self-knowledge will enquire, 'Who am I?'

Practise self-enquiry (*atma vichara*) every day, even in the moment of death. The primal error at the basis of suffering and ignorance is the wrong identification of the Self with the 'I'-thought (the ego). It goes without saying that the ego is identified with the body. The feeling of effort and struggle arises only from the thought-form, 'I am the doer.' In truth, the universe functions effortlessly.

The 'I am' that we are is not the 'I' that we believe we are. In this sense, we are a mystery to ourselves until we realize the true nature of the 'I am'. The feeling of 'I am' is more subtle than thoughts, emotions or body-awareness. Meditate constantly on the feeling of 'I am' and get free. The 'I' that is the mind-created ego cannot see the Self. However, this false 'I' can merge with or disappear into the Self. This is the destruction of the ego; this is freedom and the end of anxiety.

If 'I am' the Self, then the separation between subject and object is merely apparent, not real. Like the water of a river merging with the ocean, individual consciousness will merge with universal Consciousness through a fixed, intensive focus on the Self. This is self-enquiry.

Know your true Self. Breathe naturally. Pick any thought that appears in the mind. Silently ask the question, 'For whom is this thought?' Silently answer, 'For me.' Silently ask, 'Who am I?' Don't answer. Look for the 'I' who is asking the question. You will not find the 'I', as it is merely an apparition, a thought-form, but you will find the Self. This is the path of self-enquiry.

By actively looking for the 'I'-thought, the attention is automatically withdrawn from sense objects. The 'I'-thought, which is like a fleeting shadow, disappears the moment the light of awareness is focused on it. When the 'I'-thought vanishes, the pure Self flashes forth as an intense, silent Awareness, free of thoughts and all other phenomena. Self-enquiry is not an analysis; it is a surrendering of the intellect to the Self and the merging of the mind into Being.

Self-realization

> 'He knows bliss in the atman (Self) and wants nothing else. Cravings torment the heart; he renounces cravings. I call him illumined.'
>
> —Krishna, The Bhagavad Gita

Question: What is it like when one achieves Self-realization?
Ramana: Wrong question. One does not realize anything new.
Question: I don't get it.
Ramana: It's simple. Now you feel you are in the world. Then,

you feel that the world is in you. Attaining Self-realization is primarily a function of intention, inner purity and Grace, not mental or physical capacity. For the Self-realized, renunciation is not a vow or a positive act of renouncing, but rather the natural cessation of extraneous, misdirected activity arising from ignorance and delusion. This demands commitment and steady persistence, but not self-denial.

Impeccability is the gateway to Self-realization, hence the man of Knowledge is naturally moral and ethical, but not necessarily according to the moral and ethical standards of his time and place. The Sage refrains from moralism and judgements. For the Self-realized man or woman, there is still awareness of pain, discomfort, etc. but the Self is not identified with the body-mind, thus, there is no suffering.

Self-realization does not change the content of experience, it re-contextualizes and illumines it. No scripture or religion survives the full realization of the Self. Yet, they are not enemies and there is room for mutual respect and recognition. We may realize the Self, but we cannot change our genetics, our blueprint. We can, however, dis-identify the 'I am' from our blueprint and, correctly and directly identify the 'I am' as the Self. This demands commitment.

Seven steps to enlightenment:

1. Intention
2. Enquiry
3. Subtle mind
4. Established in truth
5. Freedom from attachments
6. Cessation of objectivity and subjectivity
7. Transcending the previous six

With enlightenment, nothing really changes. The only thing that is removed is the false identification of the Self with the body-mind and what it perceives.

Meditation

All of the religions and philosophies of the world cannot do for us what we can do for ourselves if we pause, think, reflect and most importantly, meditate. Intuitive experience is always present; the only obstacle is the overly conceptual mind. The practice of meditation will remove this obstacle. Meditation gradually extinguishes all thoughts, leaving only the quintessential Self in its perfect radiance.

When the breath is stilled, thought becomes stilled; conversely, when thought is stilled, the breath becomes stilled. Meditation stills both thought and breath. Through steady, unrelenting practice, the meditator will finally attain the extraordinary yet natural, effortless and continuous state of full Self-awareness.

Meditation is not mind-control. Forcing the mind doesn't work and is a form of repression that simply creates psychic distortion and psychosomatically induced illnesses. Concentration does not mean struggling against the mind's tendency to wander, rather it means consistently and gently bringing the mind back to the object of meditation, i.e. the *mantra* or the word or the feeling, whenever we become aware that the mind is distracted.

For the meditator, all sense of doingness melts into a pervasive feeling of beingness as the process of meditation effortlessly continues to deepen. This demands steady persistence in meditation. When the subject and object merge and become one in meditation, both disappear. What remains is the Self, by itself.

Transcendence

Transcendence is neither interior nor exterior, neither below nor above. You cannot go to transcendental Consciousness, you must beckon it, surrender to it. The silent repetition of a *mantra* or focusing on and following the breathing will be most helpful. Find someone with experience who is a qualified teacher; someone who knows this experience directly and not second-hand through lectures and books.

Yoga

The Self cannot be won by head-stands, spinal twists and salutations to the Sun, although physical stamina and mental health will improve. Yogis understand well the many uses of the breathing; nevertheless, Yoga is much more than postures and breath control.

The Yoga of Action (*karma* Yoga) combined with the Yoga of Knowledge (*jnana* Yoga) leads to freedom. *Maha Yoga* (The Great Yoga) is the knowledge that purifies the mind in preparation for liberation (*moksha*). The *Maha Yoga* of Consciousness is the real mother of all bombs—it bombs the mind with bliss and puts an end to war.

Vedanta ('The End Of Knowledge')

The system of Vedanta, which is the culmination of the Vedic knowledge, cannot be reduced to philosophy, but Vedanta and philosophy can be excellent friends. Vedanta and physics are also well-suited for each other. The great originators of quantum physics were all influenced by Vedanta. Vedanta reaches for the highest Knowledge and expresses the essence of a group of ancient Indian texts, referred to collectively as the 'Upanishads'.

Knowledge

Knowledge is different in different states of consciousness. Only the Sage truly understands this and knows how to deal with it. Everyone else argues and disagrees. That which knows can be lived but cannot be known. It is a tautology that what is known directly is what is present and what is present is what is known directly.

Conversely, what is not known directly is what is not present and what is not present is what is not known directly.

If nothing is present, then that is what is known. All other claims to knowledge are bogus, i.e. merely theoretical or speculative. Knowledge is an attribute of Consciousness. Knowledge of itself is the first and primal Knowledge of Consciousness. In this Knowledge, there is no subject and no object. All other forms of knowledge are derivative and dualistic. Knowledge means knowing, just as experience means experiencing—both knowing and experiencing exist only at the moment of Consciousness.

Without Consciousness, they disappear. Knowing and experiencing are an identity, i.e. knowing an experience, experiencing a knowing. Knowledge as ordinary knowing, involving the trinity 'knower-knowing-known' (multiplicity), is not of the same order as Knowledge as Being (singularity). Whatever is experienced, i.e. perceived, thought, felt, speculated, assumed, questioned, deduced, etc. is 'ordinary' knowledge. Ordinary knowledge appears and disappears; it has no substance, no real existence, and no permanence.

Nevertheless, knowledge has a substratum. That substratum is Consciousness. As with the Self, Consciousness is not perceived or known, yet it exists. It must exist in order for anything to be known. Knowledge is Consciousness itself.

Knowledge becomes vitiated or illusory when the mind falsely reduces the Self to a limited sphere, i.e. the body or the empirical self. Ordinary knowledge is actually ignorance, although it appears to have practical value. Within this dream called 'the waking state', there is science, birth and death, but the dream itself is not science, birth, or death. Rather, the dream appears as a function of ignorance of the Self and disappears as a function of Knowledge of the Self. This Knowledge is the Great Awakening.

5

THE MAN OF KNOWLEDGE

'Why are there beings at all, and why not rather nothing? That is the question.'
—*What is Metaphysics?*, Martin Heidegger (1889–1976)

The Sage

The insights of Sages become the subject matter of theologians and philosophers. The few words spoken by these great beings are carefully preserved and treasured by humanity. The Sages affirm that in the egoless state, there is no God (*Shiva*) who stands apart from the Self; rather, that a God who stands apart from the Self must be Himself as an entity and, ipso facto, limited. God as reality cannot be an object of thought or perception, thus, there is no such thing as an existence which is exterior to God. God is not subject to limiting factors.

The Sage enters the egoless state by the final and utter extinction of the ego—the fictitious entity which is the primary ignorance. The Sage affirms that birth is not truly birth, because we are born only to die; that death is not truly death, because we die only to be born. On the other hand, the attaining of the Natural State is true birth, because then death is dead once and for all. For the Sage, reality is a unified field without temporal or spatial boundaries in which He is included.

The Sage spoke, 'The Self is the Ocean and the world and the souls are the froth on it. To remember this always is to be firm and free from doubts and worries.' The Sage told the scholar, 'There are degrees of experience, but Reality has no degree.'

'Consciousness is not a quality; It is the very substance of Reality, and Reality is real solely because It is Consciousness. Consciousness alone exists; there is nothing else.'

—Upanishads

'To the Seer of the real Self, who is contented in the enjoyment of the Bliss of the Self, there comes without question an increase of Light, Power and Intelligence.'

—Sage Vasishtha

'That Great Intelligence which is Boundless and Radiant beyond measure, fashions thought from Its rays of light. Thought gives rise to perceptions and perceptions make up the objects of the world'

—Sage Ribhu (3000–5000 BC)

'We contemplate that Reality in which everything exists, to which everything belongs, from which everything has emerged, which is the cause of everything and which is everything.'

—Sage Vasishtha

'How can infinite Consciousness cease to be? The person is nothing but infinite Consciousness. Who dies and when, to whom does this infinite Consciousness belong and how? Even when millions of bodies die, this Consciousness exists undiminished.'

—Sage Vasishtha

The Sage speaks from his own experience and not from a knowledge of books, whether secular or scriptural. The true Sage never seeks attention, recognition or special treatment. He has no 'game plan', and he doesn't try to 'fix' the world. He is a vibrant ocean of Consciousness whose very presence is enough. The Seer does not experience himself as walking, talking or exerting any form of energy. The Seer does, however, see, hear, feel and so forth. The Sage of true Knowledge lives by Grace alone.

A Sorcerer is a master of the art of manipulating perception. A Sage, however, has realized the source of all perception and therefore has no need to manipulate. That is the difference. Those who have not realized the Self must be able to make clear distinctions in order to function in the world; the Sage also makes distinctions, but He knows they are not real and is not attached to them.

The Sage throws out the reasonable. Knowing that we have no time, He insists on a radical departure from the known that we have been brought up to believe as reality. For the Sage, there is no duality between the experience and the experiencer. They coexist as a single Being—the Self.

Ultimately, all pain is self-inflicted, stemming from self-ignorance. The Sage has no attachment to anything; therefore, he suffers no pain at the loss of anything, including his body.

> *'Only a man of non-attachment can know the power of non-attachment.'*
> —Ramana Maharshi (1879–1950)

The Sage is what He speaks of, therefore, He does not build systems of thoughts to verify what he already lives.

> *'Love itself is the actual form of God.'*
> —Ramana Maharshi (1879–1950)

> 'Those who have in this world itself attained true knowledge (jnana) in their Heart, which is beyond the knowledge of the senses, are immortals.'
>
> —Sri Muruganar (1893–1973)

The use of language always involves 'otherness'; that is why the Sage Lao Tzu wrote, 'He who knows does not speak; he who speaks does not know.'

> 'The conscious Self, remaining one, shines on all the moods of mind: on desire, determination, doubt, faith, unfaith, firmness and the lack of it, shame, insight, fear, and such as these.'
>
> —Adi Shankara (8th century AD)

The true Sages are mostly silent because they know that words and what they refer to are unreal. The Sage slowly weans his students away from illusion. He knows that if he destroys all of their illusions in one strike, they may go mad. Therefore, he is careful, compassionate and patient. Only skilfully instructed inner experience will help in attaining full realization of the Self. Every Sage understands well that the true 'Kingdom of Heaven' is the Egoless State.

Everyone has a project. Only the Sage has no need for one. People say there really are dreams, but the dreams are unreal. People say there really are objects and events in the waking state and these are real. The Sage, however, says there really are waking state objects and events and yet these things are unreal. The Sage also says that the personal God is unreal, only the Self is real and, moreover, God (*Ishwara*) and the Self are not different—all is One.

Powers

> '...everything we see, hear, feel, or in any wise perceive by sense...[is] a sign or effect of the Power of God.'
>
> —George Berkeley (1685–1753)

> *'Do not think too much of psychical phenomena and such things. Their number is legion. Clairvoyance, clairaudience, and such things are not worth having, when so much far greater illumination and peace are possible without them than with them.'*
>
> —Ramana Maharshi (1879–1950)

Ghosts, entities, spirit guides, etc.—etheric beings which appear to be separate from us are as real and as unreal as the world which appears before us every day. Divine power is not something to seek or purchase. It is already here, within us. It is us. We do not need to seek for power; we are power. It is just that we forgot. Those who seek power and dominance over others will never attain the Natural State.

Special powers such as clairvoyance and precognition come naturally as a bestowal of Grace. They cannot be attained by artifice or egoic means. Those who are attracted to the dark side should understand that the practice of black magic is spiritual suicide. So says the Sage. We will have power when we release it. When we let go of manipulation and control, power steps forth.

Reincarnation

With regard to the notion of reincarnation, the vicious circle of deaths and rebirths is sustained only by the primary ignorance which is the ego. Under the delusion of difference, the deluded soul keeps seeking new bodies, and hence, the past and future lives—the endless recycling of empirical existence. The belief in the reality of past and future is what calls forth the illusion of the reincarnation of the Self. There is no reincarnation for the Self.

Religion

> *'Turn away from all scriptures; engage in the pure Yoga of Self-realization; being convinced that nothing excels this Supreme*

> *Knowledge, hold the mind from straying.'*
> —*Atma Sakshatkara*, the Agamas

> *'Generally speaking, the errors in religion are dangerous; those in philosophy only ridiculous.'*
> —David Hume (1711–1776)

The Sages never seek to establish new religions. They only seek to release humanity from the painful devastating grip of ignorance and illusion. The religious missionary believes that his zeal for making converts is a virtue. It is not a virtue, but a vice, because his zeal is due to his egotism. He needs to convert non-believers in order to validate that he alone has the truth.

All the petty religions make great effort to impose conceptual and behavioural uniformity on humanity. This is impossible and only imposes greater pain, anguish, conflict and violence everywhere. Unfortunately, most religious teaching is like 'comfort food'. It makes us feel good for a while, but doesn't really change anything. It offers promises, but delivers very little. The Self is beyond all religions and must be known directly.

Truth

> *'Beauty is truth, truth beauty—that is all*
> *Ye know on earth, and all ye need to know.'*
> —John Keats (1795–1821)

The truth of the Self is too simple for theologians, so they write volumes about heaven and hell, good and evil, God and the Devil, my theology versus your theology. It is an endless battle among competing minds and a waste of paper. The mark of the truth-lover is that he holds his beliefs tentatively and is able to renounce them if they are found untenable. He is free from attachment to any point of view, however compelling.

'He that loves the Truth and subdues his whole being to the love of the Truth, shall find it.'
—Krishna, The Bhagavad Gita

6

THE ESSENCE OF SPIRITUALITY

Heart

'Somewhere I have never travelled, gladly beyond any experience, your eyes have their silence...'
—E.E. Cummings (1894–1962)

In the language of spirituality, Heart does not refer to the lump of flesh called by that name, but to the real Self—the original Consciousness. The Heart, which is another word for the Self, is not a *chakra* (centre of power). Everything emerges from the Heart (Self) and withdraws into the Heart. Nothing can ever leave the Heart.

Love and Compassion

So long as we perceive ourselves as isolated, we will be dominated by fear and unable to experience true empathy for others. No one owes us their love or attention, nor do we owe anyone ours. Recognizing the attention and service of others as gifts rather than obligations is a liberating insight. Love is not something we 'do'; it is our Natural State reflected in our 'doingness'. True compassion doesn't always 'look' like compassion. To the ego, the Sage can appear as the enemy.

Surrender

Freedom has no roots other than in pure Consciousness; that is why it is freedom. Give up the search for security, there is no security for the body. Such a desire is bondage. There is no security in wealth, fame or power either. Attachment and reaction feed our weaknesses; letting go and surrendering destroys them. Do not follow; do not resist; simply 'be with'.

All of this is internal and does not necessarily apply to our external actions. We should not resist doing what must be done. Sometimes we must prepare for battle, as did Prince Arjuna, under the divine guidance of Lord Krishna. The polarities of withdrawal and attachment amount to the same thing. True renunciation is an internal letting go, not an external rejection. Let the world be, do what must be done, and be kind.

Feeling

> *'I am moved by fancies that are curled*
> *Around these images, and cling: The notion of some*
> *infinitely gentle Infinitely suffering thing.'*
> —*Preludes*, T.S. Eliot (1888–1965)

Feeling is always there, it is always available. No one is left out. Look for it and you will find it. The receiving of impressions is a flowing in; the outward focusing of attention is a flowing out. Sensitive people can feel when someone is fixing their attention on them. Sometimes they feel invaded. Those who have realized the Self cannot be invaded. All of this is happening in Consciousness.

Anyone who observes animals closely will realize that they

have feelings and, though very different from human beings, are highly sensitive, intelligent and aware. Intelligence and intellect are not the same thing. There is a karmic price to pay when we abuse any living creature.

Grace

I began to awaken at seventeen, when in early winter I read John Milton's poem *Il Penseroso* and began to weep. Then, I read his *L'Allegro* and was filled with joy and hope. I had been touched by Grace. True poetry is divine, it uplifts this world; it transforms something dreary and grey into something beautiful and enchanting.

> *'One should over-come misfortunes with faith, courage and serenity, remembering that they come by God's grace, in order to give strength.'*
> —Ramana Maharshi (1879–1950)

Self-surrender invites Grace; self-aggrandizement invites trouble. The whole function of Grace is the elimination of our layers of ignorance, after which the real Self alone will remain. Grace is not special; it is truly universal; only the ego interferes. Grace is the beginning, the middle and the end, for Grace is the Self.

> *'Place all burdens on the Supreme Being and let go of anxiety. Such a courageous act of depending totally on Grace is true Devotion.'*
> —Sri Muruganar (1893–1973)

Other than through Grace, no one can truly know the Self. The ego is erased through the power of Grace, not through intellectual understanding, self-punishment or self-denial. Self-realization, which is thought to be difficult to achieve, is attained easily through the Power of Grace. It is the light of pure Consciousness that destroys the delusion of ignorance—this is the Power of Grace.

If you are already seeking to know the Self, this itself is a manifestation of Grace. Grace is essential for realization. It is given to him who has striven ceaselessly on the path of freedom.

'Grace will not combine with a bat-like (fickle) mentality.
Hold firmly and constantly to one path.'
—Sri Muruganar (1893–1973)

To be firmly established in the Heart and to know the Self through Grace is the raison d'être of our incarnation. Until one reaches the Heart, the ego will not cease. Grace is the very nature of the Supreme Being; it is omnipresent but we are too blind to see It. The lifting of the veil is Grace. Grace is the beginning, middle and end. Grace is always there. Grace is the Self.

Individually, we are incapable of Self-realization. Grace is necessary because the mind is limited. Grace is not something special, but rather universal. It is the only power for good there is. Grace is natural, but the ego interferes. Thus, the ego must be abandoned. Affirm, 'By Divine Grace, there is neither distress, nor fear, nor illness, nor decay, for Me.'

Throughout all the various transformations in our varied lives, we have been 'Graced' with glimpses of the underlying unity behind all appearances. This unity is the unchanging reality. The revelation of Being to man is called Grace. Grace cannot be hunted down, it finds us. Faith, on the other hand, is a choice, a decision, an operation of the mind and emotions. Those imbued with Grace are endowed with a magnetic power of attraction. After much self-effort, one attains direct Knowledge of the Self, but this final step is by divine Grace alone.

Vision

True vision is not ordinary looking or seeing, nor is it imagination or dreaming. It is not even a product of rationality, logic or common sense. Vision arises from a place within us that is deeper than the intellect, deeper than emotion, and beyond perception. Vision is natural; it is the absence of vision that causes an abnormal condition.

7

OUR DESCRIPTION OF THE WORLD

'There is in truth no cause, no result, and no action; all that is chimerical. There is no world and no dweller in it. The Universe has no external support, nor is it cognized from without; but as you make it so it becomes.'
—*Devikalottara*, the Agamas

The World as Description

The world we see is an interpretation—'our' interpretation. The raw data of the senses, including that raw data perceived through a telescope or a microscope, will never tell us the answer to the ontological questions of free will versus predetermination, or infinity versus finiteness, etc. In these instances, we are reduced to probabilities, possibilities, theories and assumptions. There will never be a final and empirical proof because the external world starts as an interpretation and develops from there. The world is a description that is gradually built-up in our mind, but the mind cannot conceive what is happening at the ends of the universe or even if there is, indeed, a beginning or an end to the universe of which this world is an extraordinarily minuscule part.

The building of our description of the world allows the process of reflection—actually, it demands it. To reflect is to think about. A memory is a recollection of an already reflected upon object or event, i.e. something significant that we take note of. Even the very young engage in reflection, otherwise they would never mature.

Our descriptions refer to something other than themselves. Descriptions can also refer to other descriptions. Descriptions may also be self-referring (e.g., an artist painting a picture of himself painting a picture of himself). In essence, a description is always an interpretation of something other than itself. The true nature or reality of what is being described is never fully realized by description. Descriptions are like maps, they help us navigate a terrain but they never give us full knowledge of the actual landscape.

Descriptions can be relatively true, relatively false or relatively muddled. There can be no other absolute description of anything other than itself. Description is not that which is being described. Words, which make up the bulk of description, are sounds, and as sounds, they are energy. This energy is heard by virtue of Consciousness. Words are also meaning, and as meaning, they are Consciousness. Meaning only exists as meaning in Consciousness. Descriptions exist as descriptions only in Consciousness. The words 'energy' and 'matter' refer to something other than themselves. As words, they are sounds, i.e. energy, but as meaning, they are intelligence, i.e. Consciousness.

The information stored in a computer, book or a calculation device is meaningless in the absence of Consciousness. Strangely, Consciousness can never observe itself. Therefore, it can never be described or even proven. Yet, Its reality is undeniable. This is the great mystery.

Appearance

Appearance is always an appearance of some-'thing', but it is not the thing itself. What we call an 'object' is neither truly separate nor distinct. It only appears to be so. Thus, the object that is perceived is unreal in any sense other than as an appearance. The apparent object exists only so long as it is perceived. What we call the world or the body are the 'world-appearance' and the 'body-appearance'. Does a world or a body exist independently of its appearance? There is no way to prove this. We can only infer it. And if it does exist, its true reality must be vastly different from its appearance.

The world-appearance exists only as an appearance. It also represents something else—something hidden. But it is not that which it represents. Thus, we say that it has no real existence in itself, other than as an appearance. Being merely a limited reflection of something else—something mysterious—it is similar to a magic show. The Sage, however, does not deny the reality of what the appearance is reflecting, whatever that reality may or may not be.

All that is finite and relative is an appearance that appears and melts away, its seeming reality constantly revealing itself as unreal. Appearance is a limited manifestation of infinite Consciousness. What is hidden beneath the appearance is vibrant Consciousness (*Shakti*). That power may assume a form appearing to be solid and finite, but this does not mean that what is being revealed is, in fact, solid or finite. Appearances have their being in Consciousness and are a reflection of power (*Shakti*). This power is inherent in pure Consciousness, hence the term, 'The Power of Consciousness'.

External World

What we call the 'external world' is simply power (*Shakti*), and power is not an object, a thing or 'things'. Our belief in an external world is what deludes us into taking the world-appearance to be real, just as our belief in a pool of water in the desert deludes us into believing that the mirage is real. This illusion persists as long as we confuse appearance with reality. The external world is a mystery, yet it is something we must assume for pragmatic reasons. If we do not treat the external world as something real, we will suffer extraordinary hardship. For those who are on the path, yet not Self-realized, this is a necessary paradox that must be respected.

There is neither 'something' nor 'nothing' exterior to Consciousness. How could there be? Pure Consciousness is not in physical, however subtle that physicality may be, as in the case of ether (*akasha*). In the waking state, our senses appear to be in contact with the external world. The same is true of the dream state. But appearances are not reality. We are never looking at an external world; such a world is merely theoretical. Or we are only looking at an external world which we perceive to be external to our physical body.

However, this is not fundamentally different from regarding any two objects within our description, such as an apple and an orange, as external to each other. Our body, which 'we' perceive, is equally external to the apple as is the orange external to the apple. All these relative externalities—the apple, the orange, our body—compose a large part of our description of the world. Our primordial ontological error as a species is to assume that the Self we are is identical with or belongs to the body. This is a wrong assumption for which we pay a heavy price.

The Seer, whose true nature is Consciousness, sees equally the body, the apple and the orange as three distinct objects. Given this, how can we assume that the Seer belongs to the body alone? The body cannot simultaneously be an object as well as its own witnessing subject (the Seer), just as the sculptured object, 'David', cannot be the witnessing subject of its sculptor, Michelangelo. 'David' has a body and appears to have eyes that see and ears that hear, but David sees and hears naught, for there is no 'subject' living exclusively inside of David.

Simply put, the subject cannot be its own object while remaining the subject. The contradiction resides in the false assumption that the witnessing subject belongs to the body. It does not. Consciousness is a different order of reality from the insentient matter which composes the gross body. The body provides the senses that process the data that are reflected in Consciousness, but the data are neither the witness nor the appearance. Rather, 'data' belong to the insentient matter which composes the body, similar to the data stored and processed in a (insentient) computer. And, just as with a computer, the 'data' stored in our human bodies remain unknown until they are reflected in Consciousness. It is Consciousness and Consciousness alone who is the 'Seer' of data.

Appearance, along with all of its content including the body-image, belongs to Consciousness, while 'data' belongs to the assumed, hidden and unproven 'in-itself', i.e. the 'body' behind the appearance. And just as appearance belongs to Consciousness, Consciousness belongs to the Self—appearance does not belong to the body. If the Self is all-embracing, then there can be nothing external to it. If there is nothing external, there is nothing internal to it either.

That which is beyond all relativity is relationless. Thus, to an enlightened Sage who knows Himself only as the Self, there is no external world nor is there an internal world. However, to ordinary humanity, which wrongly identifies the Self as belonging to the body, there is no doubt about the reality of external and internal worlds. Thus is humanity imprisoned and deluded by ignorance.

Reality

The ever-changing world has its being in reality, but reality itself never undergoes real change. The senses and the intellect cannot turn back on their source in order to observe it; nor will they ever observe it, for it is not observable. Nevertheless, it can be known directly, without the false subject-object duality.

Some say, 'This world we see, though constantly changing, must be real.' In truth, however, changelessness is a fundamental attribute of reality, change itself being merely a flow of appearances similar to the play of light on a stationary movie screen or a flow of currents moving within a body of water. In both instances, neither the screen nor the body of water are altered by the play of images or the moving currents.

Whatever absorbs our attention, whether rational or nonsensical, appears to be real but is not. In order to keep the world-movie going, we must believe that the movie is real and not a mere movie; we must become expert in self-deception; we must remain serious and self-important.

All forms of ignorance are unreal. Ignorance is the absence of reality. There is no such thing as 'real' ignorance, rather, ignorance is a pure 'negation' similar to the numbing and covering effect of anesthesia. Reality is what it is. Neither ignorance nor empirical knowledge can alter reality, and like the antics of both bad and good actors on a stage, nothing really happens.

A description of reality is not reality; description does not belong to reality but to the knower. The knower himself is also included in the description and is thus not reality. The importance we attach to the ever-changing world-appearance of objects and events is unimportant, except that it keeps us occupied and deluded. Reality only 'appears' to undergo change. This is the great delusion. This delusion, which belongs exclusively to ourselves, is the source of our suffering and bewilderment.

All philosophy is an attempt to describe reality, but reality is not a description and it cannot be described. Description, however, is included in reality and since description has no independent existence, it is, therefore, by itself unreal. The world and reality are negations of each other. Why? Because the world that we know is a world of appearances—appearances occurring within

Consciousness. Appearances disappear during deep sleep, but the Being—the Self—remains. It is the Self, the Being-Consciousness, that is the enduring substratum underlying appearances, rather than an inferred external world laying on the other side of what is revealed in Consciousness.

Pure Consciousness is the substratum of all that is revealed and hidden, manifest and unmanifest, real and false—in short, of all polarities. Even our body is a part of the world-appearance, being a composite of appearances experienced during the waking state and vanishing with the onset of deep sleep. The term 'reality' implies 'that which endures'. But our world of appearances does not endure nor are we guaranteed that appearances of specific objects, such as distant trees, bodies of water, etc. are reliable.

Also, the organism is vulnerable to loss of memory, delusion, madness, as well as sensory distortion due to disease and accident, etc. Thus, we can be easily mistaken or deceived. The only world we know is the world as it appears to us and these appearances are often proven false, as when what we see turns out to be a mirage or a fantasy or a psychological delusion.

Name and Form

Form is activity; activity is form. Form is never static, although it may appear to be. Form undergoes constant transformation, and therefore, form is not exactly real and not exactly unreal. Form itself is a manifestation of the power of Consciousness, but it is the power of Consciousness 'within' the form that is real.

Form is not substance, yet substance inhabits form. Pure Consciousness is the primal essence of substance and, by the power of *Shakti* inherent within Consciousness, substance takes its first manifestation as the extremely subtle '*akasha*' (ether). This primal manifestation of ether is more subtle than ordinary matter, and more subtle than any proposed 'finest particle'.

Space inheres in form, but form does not inhere in space; the same is true of the Self. The Self is everywhere and nowhere; it is not spread out like a blanket. Whatever we conceive the Self to be, 'that' is not it. We meditate on form in order to transcend it. Name and form are not substances. Thus, a bracelet of a certain shape is gold, but gold is not a bracelet. Name and form is something we assign to what appears to be stable but which in reality is not. Illusion is assigning substance or permanence to that which is neither.

Form is constantly changing; it is the play of energy. Unlike form, energy is neither created nor destroyed. Energy has its being in Consciousness. Pure and real space is a 'potentiality' until it begins to transform into material space. The same principle applies to *Shakti* (power) and its manifestation, *prana* (vital force, energy). *Prana* manifests as 'name and form', meaning, all of the ever-changing organic and inorganic entities which comprise the universe.

Illusion (Maya)

> *'Unreal City,*
> *Under the brown fog of a winter dawn,*
> *A crowd flowed over London Bridge, so many, I had not thought death had undone so many. Sighs, short and infrequent, were exhaled, and each man fixed is eyes before his feet.'*
>
> —*The Wasteland*, T.S. Eliot (1888–1965)

We begin life with the belief that happiness can be had in and through what this world has to offer. And most people go on believing this for a very long time. It is the Great Delusion. It is also true that service, as opposed to acquisition, brings a feeling of beatitude. What this world has to offer is the opportunity to serve. If the world is simply because it appears so to our senses, then a blue mirage in a hot, barren desert must be water. That which is transitory is illusory. Time past and time future is *Maya* (illusion)—remove time and there is no *Maya*. History, which is time, is illusory—it is a dialogue that poorly imitates reality.

The unmanifested Power of *Maya* (illusion) exists in the Self and is not separate from it. *Maya*, manifested, is a negation—a non-existence, unreal. *Maya* is the great deception that keeps us spinning endlessly on the wheel of birth and death. The world we believe to be separate from Consciousness is an illusory world, and the world we see as having its being in Consciousness is a real world—it is as real as Consciousness itself. The real world is not in any sense separate from its source.

Once a delusion is recognized, it disappears. Once something real is recognized, it continues. If, as by magic, the blue body of water in the burning desert should disappear, it was a delusion, something merely imagined. When all delusion is removed, what remains is the pure light of the Self. The play of Power (*Shakti*) creates the illusion of 'thing-ness', because what appears to be substantial and enduring, i.e. material objects, is merely flux. *Maya* is the illusion that something which is not, 'is'. This is called the 'sport' of the Supreme Being, but in our ignorance, we take this sport to be reality. Our ignorance is also the sport of the Supreme.

Thus, we falsely believe that we are independent and separate from Him. Our primary purpose in this life is to remove the blanket of ignorance from our eyes and awaken to our true nature. In reality, there is no true 'other-ness'—all is One. Illusion (*Maya*) is a false appearance; it is that which does not exist, yet appears to.

> *'There is no unreal thing that has an unreality as its cause; similarly there is no unreal thing that has reality as its cause. Moreover, there is no existing thing that has another existing thing as its cause. How can there be an unreal thing that is produced out of something real?'*
> —Gaudapada (8th century AD)

The illusion of a duality of knower and known creates disequilibrium. When the dual 'knower-known' is resolved into a singular 'knowing-ness', then disequilibrium disappears.

Maya is the beginningless cause that manifests as the illusion of a world that is both different and separate from the Self.

8

COUNTERING SCIENTIFIC MATERIALISM

Science

'Since the theory of general relativity implies the representation of physical reality by a continuous field, the concept of particles or material points cannot play a fundamental part, nor can the concept of motion.'

—Albert Einstein (1879–1955)

The German physicist Werner Heisenberg established that the act of observation or measurement affects the phenomenon being observed or measured. He wrote, 'What we observe is not nature in itself but nature exposed to our method of questioning.' In other words, the result is always tainted by the enquiry itself. With this insight, he formulated his famous 'indeterminacy principle' which demolished the cherished notion of the scientist as a detached, objective observer. The world we see is basically a creation of our own way of thinking, asking and perceiving. Doesn't it make more sense to first know the thinker, questioner and perceiver?

Instead, what we do is assume that what we perceive is the world as it actually is and then proceed to act on that assumption.

Reputedly, science is based solely on objectivity. This is false. The false, egoistic nature of the experiencing subject is the Achilles heel of science. The scientist is never manipulating 'things'; he is manipulating energy. In reality, he is playing with fire. Is he truly competent? This is the fundamental question we must ask?

Materialism

> '... *unlike the self imagined by the logicians, the Self is not to be established by the mere means of the human intellect.*'
> —Adi Shankara (8th century AD)

Scientific materialism often asserts that Consciousness is an 'epiphenomenon'* of insentient matter. Nothing could be further from the truth. Some materialist philosophers assert, 'If there is no "consciousness of…", then there is no consciousness.' But the Sage says, 'If there is no Consciousness, then there is no "consciousness of…"' If it is true that Consciousness is an epiphenomenon of the brain, then Consciousness must be biological in nature. But then, how can something which is immaterial and non-perceivable, such as Consciousness, be said to be biological?

What is produced from matter/energy/action must be of the nature of matter/energy/action. However, Consciousness is neither matter nor energy nor action, and we cannot observe or measure it. Consciousness is truly intangible yet there is a common materialist assumption that it is produced by a body that is itself tangible and measurable. This assumption is obvious and convenient, but when examined more closely, we see it is not sound and has never been established empirically.

Knowledge demands Consciousness, for without it, nothing

---

*'Epiphenomenon' (def.): a secondary effect or byproduct that arises from but does not causally influence a process: specifically, brain activity.

can be known. If Consciousness is an epiphenomenon of biology, then by its nature, it must be material and therefore observable. But Consciousness, like knowledge and light, is not observable. Brain waves are observable, but they do not tell us what the actual content of experience is. What we know directly is private, as is Consciousness. We can describe what we know to others, yet what we are passing on is not our direct experience, but rather a description of it. Consciousness is even more elusive than knowledge because it is formless, weightless and invisible.

None of the five senses have access to it and unlike ordinary knowledge, Consciousness cannot be transmitted to others even in the form of a description (other than to say that it is indescribable). Yet, Consciousness is real.

It exists, because whatever its exact nature is, we cannot deny it. Appearance demands Consciousness, but Consciousness does not demand appearance. Consciousness is the substratum underlying all knowledge and experience. For this reason, Consciousness has primacy.

Matter and Substance

> *'...space is demonstrated to exist through inference.'*
> —Adi Shankara (8th century AD)

> *'The notion that all these fragments are separately existent is evidently an illusion, and this illusion cannot do other than lead to endless conflict and confusion. Indeed, the attempt to live according to the notion that the fragments are really separate is, in essence, what has led to the growing series of extremely urgent crises that is confronting us today.'*
> —David Bohm (1917–1992)

> *'The only thing whose existence we deny is that which 'philosophers' call Matter or corporeal substance.'*
> —George Berkeley (1685–1753)

We believe we see matter and energy, but what is really 'there', is Consciousness. All forms of matter, subtle or gross, are simply *Shakti* (power), manifesting as *prana* (primal force). That substance which is involved in time and space has its being in that which is neither substance, time nor space, but transcends all three and is infinitely greater—pure Consciousness.

All matter is in a state of continual change, and therefore, all matter is always in a state of becoming, i.e. becoming something else, hence transformation. All becoming occurs within Being, which in itself remains eternally as it is—limitless, borderless and free. Whatever appears substantial, i.e. the material objective universe, is in reality, insubstantial. The illusion of substantiality is a manifestation of the deluding Power of *Maya*. Remove substance and there is no such impression of either time or space or space-time. The impression of time and space is clearly a function of the apparent relationships among apparently discrete objects and events.

Clay is the material cause of all objects made of clay. All varieties of clay pots and figurines are simply clay. Here, the term 'clay' is used as an analogy for the Power of Consciousness (*Chit-Shakti*). Thus, the infinite variety of forms which are manifested from *Chit-Shakti* remain simply *Chit-Shakti*, regardless of their structure. All sensorially determined duality is merely relative. In reality, there is no duality. There is undoubtedly a manifest level of subtle essence (*akasha*) that may remain forever beyond our ability to perceive. This super-fine, subtle essence is not different from Being-Consciousness.

Material space has its being in transcendental space. The first and most subtle manifestation of material space is *akasha* (ether). With the progressive manifestation of material space, arises name, form and apparent discreteness. From discreteness (objectivity, 'thingness'), arise the notions of time, distance, causality and mass. Matter/energy (*prana*) is always in perfect equilibrium with the present moment, which is the only moment that is. Nothing is really happening. The mind has difficulty accepting this.

The universe is simply intelligence masquerading as matter. In our ignorance, we buy into the illusion that matter is real. Even though renowned as a mystic and Seer, the Sage Adi Shankara's philosophy is significantly empirical. Whatever can be observed is of the nature of matter. The totality of matter is called the Field (*kshetra*). Thoughts, feelings, ideas and intelligence are attributes of the organism and are therefore material, albeit subtle. According to Shankara, the knower of the field of matter is not itself material nor in any sense dependent on matter.

Rather, the knower is the Self or pure Consciousness. The knower is utterly immaterial and therefore, not observable, measurable or in any way, empirically verifiable. Thus, it is not accessible to science or subject to any of its modalities. Shankara also upheld the *advaitic* (non-dualist) view that the field (*kshetra*) is not different from the Self (*atman*); that the Self is not different from the Creator (*Shiva*); and, that the Creator is not different from the Supreme, Absolute Being (*Brahman*). In other words, the 'material' universe has its being in Consciousness.

Empiricism

> 'The empirical basis of objective science has...nothing "absolute" about it. Science does not rest upon solid bedrock. The bold structure of its theories rise, as it were above a swamp.'
> —Sir Karl Popper (1902–1994)

> 'There are more things in heaven and earth, Horatio, than are dreamt of in your philosophy.'
> —*Hamlet*, William Shakespeare (1564–1616)

At the basis of all of our empirical problems lies an ontological* problem and an ontological solution. The notion of Consciousness

---

*'Ontology' (def.): study of the metaphysics of the nature of Being.

presents a great challenge to the empirical sciences, since it is not directly observable or measurable. As it is non-sensuous, its existence is actually beyond the scope of empiricism to either affirm or deny. Paradoxically, even the most hardcore empiricist will admit that in the absence of Consciousness, he cannot think about, discuss or investigate anything.

Being-Consciousness—the Self—is not accessible to empiricism and scientific method. It may be inferred, but ultimately, must be directly experienced as a non-sensual reality. Such experience will always remain private to the knower. Empirical knowledge also has its being in the Self because Consciousness is the substratum of all empirical enquiry.

Empirical space—the space of science—is a manifestation of energy (*Shakti*). But it is not so with transcendental space. Just as the universe may expand and contract, empirical space may do the same.

Transcendental space includes empirical space as Being, which is itself limitless; neither moving nor unmoving, neither contracting nor expanding. Empirical space can be conceived, but not the space of Being.

The empiricist affirms that the blue body of water in the distant desert is a mirage and does not exist, while the body of water that he can taste and touch with his tongue and hands does exist and is not an illusion. In reality, however, both the mirage and the actual body of water are appearances. A man dying of thirst, of course, prefers the second appearance!

The Finest Particle

'What we observe as material bodies and forces are nothing but shapes and variations in the structure of space. Particles are just appearances. The world is given to me only once, not one existing and one perceived. Subject and object are only one.

The barrier between them cannot be said to have broken down as a result of recent experience in the physical sciences, for this barrier does not exist.
—Erwin Schrödinger (1887–1961)

The field of the Higgs-Boson* is extremely subtle and has been difficult to verify empirically. There are undoubtedly limits to empirical method. There may be a limit beyond which the technology of scientific enquiry cannot reach.

Particles are mere appearance; there is no such 'thing-in-itself' as a particle. The notion of a finest particle is false—there are only appearances of points becoming waves, *ad infinitum*. There are no finest, enduring subatomic particles, only extremely subtle, subatomic events that may briefly appear as points.

Subject and Object

'...consciousness of another, of an object in general, is in fact... self-consciousness, reflectedness in self, consciousness of oneself in one's other.'
—Georg Wilhelm Friedrich Hegel (1770–1831)

There are two types of non-abstract objects—objects in Consciousness and inferred objects. The first is revealed as an appearance; the second, as an inferred possibility based on evidence revealed by appearance. There is no subject witnessing an object, there is only 'appearances appearing'—subject and object cannot be separated.

The Self is a transcendental space as well as a material space, albeit material space is insentient whereas transcendental space is pure Consciousness. The 'object'-thing itself does not appear to be conscious (e.g., a rock or a hand) even though it

---

*'Higgs-Boson' (def.): a theoretical subatomic particle whose existence has been predicted by the theory that unified the weak and electromagnetic interactions.

is permeated by and has its being in Consciousness. Material space, although insentient, is manifested by the Power inherent in Consciousness (*Shakti*). From this insentient material space, arise sentient material organisms. There is no duality between Consciousness and *Shakti*.

Objects, as both organic and inorganic forms, may manifest insentience, yet they too have their being in Consciousness. Everything everywhere has its ultimate being in Consciousness. This limitless intelligence permeates and enfolds the entire cosmos. The object known is identical with the knower. They are a tautology. When there is nothing known, there is no knower and vice versa. Whatever the known or the unknown is, it exists—it exists within existence itself.

An object is revealed in Consciousness as an idea created out of a collection of perspectives and subject to continual change. Solipsism demands a subject (the ego) in order to know an object. The Self demands no subject and no object. I am the Self. I am neither the subject nor the object, thus, there is no me, you or it. All is One—Being-Consciousness-Bliss (*Sat-Chit-Ananda*).

An object hides the impressions of which it is composed, just as impressions hide the object which they compose—a strange paradox that depends upon our point of view, literally. We cannot focus on the impressions and the object at the same moment. The picture below shows two faces, but the viewer cannot see both faces simultaneously. However, the impressions which compose the two faces remain the same. Notice how the young woman's ear is the old woman's eye; how her necklace is the old woman's mouth, and how her chin is the old woman's nose.

We cannot see both at once, even though we are always looking at the same set of impressions. Which picture is real? The answer is both and neither. So, it is with every-'thing', i.e. 'object', that we see, touch, hear, taste and smell. We never perceive the 'thing' as it actually is.

Young woman, old woman. Which one is real?

When we look directly into the subject, the object disappears. Strangely, the subject also disappears. Why? Because the subject was never there in the first place. We perceive the object because we focus on it. When we shift our focus away from the object and towards the subject, we lose the object, but we lose the observing subject as well. Again, why? Because there is no actual observing subject within us that is looking out towards the object.

If we turn our attention away from the object and towards the observer, we discover that the 'observer' doesn't really exist. It is the impression of an object that creates the sense of an observer, but when we look for the observer we can't find it. What we may find are thoughts and feelings, which are simply subtle objects, but we still haven't found the subject. So long as we have either a gross or a subtle object to focus on, we will still 'feel' that there is an observer.

In reality, there is no such thing as an object-subject duality. The observer and the observed appear and disappear together.

Neither subject nor object will survive without the other; they cannot be separated. This sense of duality is an illusion. Is there really an external world? Is there really an internal subject viewing it? Can anything, subject or object, exist independently of Consciousness? The answer is 'No'—Consciousness is the substratum of all experience.

In reality, there is no such 'thing' as an observer, and when we look for it, we momentarily find ourselves in a silent space of awareness within which there is nothing to observe. At this level, what remains is Consciousness alone, and Consciousness is neither that which is observed nor that which observes. Rather, Consciousness is the screen upon which the dance of observer and observed unfolds. By its very appearance, an object—any object—establishes the fact of Consciousness.

The search for the 'observer' has also been called 'self-enquiry'. Through persistent self-enquiry, the true undying Self will be realized. The object always affirms the 'I', for without an object, the 'I' disappears. The reverse is also true. Subject and object rise and fall together. In deep sleep, the object does not exist, nor does the 'I' that knows it. They return simultaneously upon awakening.

Both the object and the subject are not different from Consciousness; they neither add to nor take away from Consciousness. There is consciousness of 'I' (the agent) and consciousness of 'it' (the object), yet neither are the Self. Nevertheless, both have their being in the Self. We can never step outside of Consciousness in order to determine whether something independent of Consciousness exists. Pleasure demands an object and is bound; true bliss has no object and is free.

9

POWER

> 'The mere consciousness of being as Awareness is itself 'Shakti', and all this world is a projection of this Shakti. The true state of Knowledge is that in which the mind is not attached to this Shakti.'
>
> —*Devikalottara*, the Agamas

Shakti and Prana

Shakti, the Power inherent within the Absolute, manifests as *prana*. *Prana* is the totality of all energy—the bioenergy of all life forms; the motor power of the mind-stuff; the primal force of the universe. Whatever exists and manifests is *prana* in one form or another. Appearances (phenomena) are like the two sides of a coin—one side is pure Consciousness, while the other side is energy/matter.

However, there is an important distinction between the two sides. Remove Consciousness and energy/matter will disappear; remove energy/matter and Consciousness will still be there. Why? Because energy/matter is relative and, ultimately, dependent on

Consciousness, whereas Being-Consciousness is Absolute and Self-sustaining.

Dense configurations of energy appear to be insentient, nevertheless, energy (*prana*) has its being in Consciousness. Bliss is more than absolute stillness; it is also closely associated with *Shakti* (power). Thus, it implies expression, bursting forth, creative impulse, i.e. life itself. *Shakti* (power) resides in Being-Consciousness. It manifests as *prana* (vital and primal force).

All the elements (earth, fire, water, air, ether) manifest from *Shakti* (power). Nothing is static in the universe; the universe is dynamic. The universe emerges and vibrates because of vital and primal force (*prana*); the whole Creation is pulsating with *prana* as its engine and support. *Prana* manifests as both the gross physical body and the subtle etheric body, which together comprise the totality of the organism (body and soul). There is a correlation between the fullness and fluidity of our breath and our physical and emotional well-being. Both are upheld by *prana*.

The breath is the link that binds the gross and the subtle aspects of the organism together. When we take our final breath on Earth, our physical functions stop, yet we remain in our subtle, etheric form. *Prana*—the vital, primal force—never sleeps and is beyond the grasp of death. When our body dies, the subtle vital force simply departs. Who are we? The gross and subtle bodies mirror each other. The Self simply 'is', with or without the adjuncts of these two bodies. The gross and subtle bodies are relative; the Self is absolute and immortal—the Self is pure Consciousness.

For the Sage, the Universe is simply power. Power is neither created nor destroyed. Power is nothing; it is no-'thing'. Power is pervaded by Consciousness and is not different from it. Physical space (*akasha*) is the first manifestation of power. Power has its being in Consciousness.

The creative power of *Shakti* includes the deluding power of *Maya* (illusion). The Self is the transcendental source of both, yet is neither *Shakti* nor *Maya*. The quintessential Self is pure Consciousness alone. Our human consciousness is a pale reflection of pure Consciousness. We have vastly more power and potential awareness than we know. There are no real objects, only power appearing as objects.

From the microscopic to the macrocosmic, power itself is fluid, only seeming to take the form of discrete objects. What appears to be a vast array of objects and events within physical space is really just 'lumpiness' manifesting and unmanifesting within the plenum of Being-Consciousness, the Self.

The potential for cognition inherent in *Shakti* is, by extension, inherent in the Self; leading to the evolution of organisms with the apparatus for cognition, such as the nervous system, the sense organs, etc. *Shakti*, when manifest as organic life, is termed *prana* (life force, vital force). The two are really one. *Shakti* is also termed *prana* (primal force) when it manifests as inorganic insentient matter. No two moments are exactly the same since power is never static.

However subtle the substance, there is always movement, currents, exchanges and so forth, occurring. The dynamism of power is always manifesting now. Power has neither a past nor a future; nor does Consciousness; nor does the Self; nor do you or I. What we call energy really is *Shakti* (potential) or *prana* (kinetic). Matter is also *prana*. Thus, the universe is only power appearing as matter/energy.

The Big Bang, if there was one, is a primal manifestation of *Shakti*. Before the Big Bang, there was only luminous silence. *Shakti* has its being in pure Consciousness. Pure Consciousness transcends *Shakti*. *Shakti* is the Power of Consciousness and manifests as *prana*. When *Shakti* withdraws and returns to its unmanifest state of pure potentiality, Consciousness remains as it is—luminous and transcendent.

Manifestation, which is power (*Shakti*), is flux. Other than the Self, there is no permanence. Forms may appear to be stable, but this is an illusion created by the limitations of the physical senses and the intellect. Even the hardest diamond is simply power—its solidity is relative, not absolute.

> *'Recognition of the world as the manifestation of Shakti is worship of Shakti. Pure Knowledge, unrelated to objects, is absolute.'*
>
> —*Devikalottara*, the Agamas

The universe is immaterial; it is simply fields of force which are structured in Consciousness. Maya is the play of *Shakti*. Both are held within Consciousness. The Being of Consciousness is revealed through *Shakti*. We are able to grasp, in a limited sense, the 'dance' of *Shakti*. Consciousness is Being—it is Being-Consciousness. Power has its being in Consciousness: it is a manifestation of Being-Consciousness. This manifestation of power clouds or obscures the essential nature of Being-Consciousness. Why? Because until we Self-realize, knowledge of the manifest is always accompanied by its polar opposite, ignorance.

The intentional 'I' is fictitious. There is only the play of power, and the relative, intentional 'I' is not the source of this. Thus, we struggle unnecessarily. Being-Consciousness is not a form of *prana*, It is the very essence of *prana*. Intentional consciousness is *prana*, which has its being in non-intentional, pure Consciousness. The transition is a function of *Shakti*.

Consciousness is the source of will (Intention). Will is *Shakti*; it inheres as potentiality in pure Consciousness. Consciousness is quality-less and yet it exists. It is the source of intentionality and intentionality is a manifestation of *Shakti*. Intentionality has its being in Consciousness.

Pure energy in the form of physical space (ether) is the first manifestation of Consciousness. Energy as 'forms' within space is the second manifestation and appears to be different from Consciousness. This appearance is an illusion (*Maya*). All forms (and their names) have their being in Consciousness. *Prana* is the material source of all organic life, both visible and invisible.

Therefore, *prana* is also not different from the Self.

The life force (*prana*) involves both power (*Shakti*) and Consciousness (*Chit*). There is no duality among these three; they are One (*Chit-Shakti*). At the heart of every material 'thing', there is *Shakti* and at the heart of *Shakti* is Being-Consciousness. The potential intentionality inherent in Consciousness manifests as a form of *prana*. Manifest or unmanifest, intentionality never leaves its Source.

In whatever form *prana* expands and contracts, it never leaves its Source—pure Consciousness. Consciousness always remains as it is— luminous, boundless and transcendent. At the heart of every material thing (sentient or insentient), there is *Shakti-prana* and at the heart of *Shakti-prana* is Being-Consciousness, i.e. the Self.

Energy is nothing, i.e. it is no-'thing'. Energy is not substance, but appears as substance. Like fire, energy must be handled carefully and with respect. Energy and ignorance combined create havoc and pain. A strong, organic manifestation of *prana* is like honey, it can attract vermin. Therefore, men and women with generous hearts and great vitality, indicating a potent degree of life force, must be cautious.

Vibration

What we call an object or event is simply movement, and movement is simply vibration appearing to be solid or actual. What appears actual is, in fact, the flux or vibration arising within Being-Consciousness. There is no solidity or substance to vibration. Consciousness, while itself neither moving nor unmoving, permeates vibration and appears to be vibrating as subject and object. This is a false superimposition.

From vibration, emanates nature, which is permeated by the Self and is not different from the Self. Appearance is a function of vibration arising in Consciousness. Vibration of light and sound gives rise to a worldview that allows the ego to locate itself in time and space. Vibration and Consciousness are not distinct, they are inseparable, yet pure Consciousness transcends even vibration. The Self is beyond knowing and acting, yet is the Source of the principle of vibration. The manifest universe is kinetic energy and has its being in pure Consciousness.

10

THE PRIMACY OF CONSCIOUSNESS
Pure Consciousness

'Consciousness itself is...
...The still point of the turning world...'
—T.S. Eliot (1888–1965)

The one incontrovertible reality is Awareness itself, by itself. Awareness stands alone and unsupported. We are that Awareness. Consciousness can never become unconscious; It is the unchanging substratum of the waking, dreaming and sleeping states. All worlds are private to their beholders, however, what unites these worlds is not name or form or substance, but the pure Consciousness that underlies all diverse experience.

I cannot think of anything that has greater primacy than Consciousness itself. Why? Because Consciousness is the foundation of all experience and in the absence of experience, all that remains is void. Consciousness is the witness of the body-mind and its actions. Consciousness is also the witness of the physical universe. Consciousness is not itself located in time and space, rather time and space have their being in Consciousness.

In order to disprove Consciousness, there must be Consciousness, which is absurd. Consciousness does not act on itself. There is no such thing as a cognition of a cognition or a perception of a perception. Any cognition is knowledge and there is no possibility of an infinite regression. The problem of infinite regression applies only to a peculiar language called 'logic'.

Perceptions and cognitions are never static, they are in a constant state of transformation, however subtle. To all this, Consciousness remains as the unchanging witness. This unchanging witness of cognition and perception is not a 'thing' that can be perceived. It is the transcendent substratum of ever-changing phenomena. We say, 'The Sun is shining', but the only thing that is truly shining is Consciousness. In the absence of Consciousness, the light goes out. The light of the Sun illumines the Moon, but it is the light of Consciousness that illumines the light of the Sun.

The Sun reveals itself by its very light, the same light by which we perceive. So it is with the Self. Without the light of the Consciousness, there is no light of the Sun. Consciousness illuminates sunlight, but sunlight does not illuminate Consciousness. Therefore, Consciousness is more subtle and more powerful.

Consciousness-without-an-object is 'Self-awareness'; consciousness-of-an-object is 'other-awareness'. Self-awareness is inherent in other-awareness, although it is habitually overlooked due to the mind's fixation on objective experience. 'Other-awareness' is fleeting and absolutely dependent on pure Consciousness. 'Consciousness-of-something' is fundamentally different from 'Consciousness-as-the-Self'.

Not knowing Consciousness as the ultimate Supreme truth of ourselves is a special form of ignorance and not merely a false idea or belief. The erroneous superimposition of the body/mind-stuff on the true Self confuses the body with the Self and wrongly reduces Consciousness to a temporal epiphenomenon of the body's biochemistry. This is the most fundamental error of scientific materialism.

Pure Consciousness is content-less and, as content-less, it does not reveal itself to itself as Consciousness. It is clear that the brain and Consciousness have a direct relationship in the manifestation of appearances, but we cannot assume that this relationship is a causal one, in the sense of one 'causing' the other, directly or indirectly. Nevertheless, the brain, born of *Shakti*, has its ultimate being in Consciousness.

Consciousness makes its appearance as matter, without becoming matter. There is no such thing as matter, since there is no such thing as a finest particle. Pure Consciousness is spontaneously Self-aware. It has direct non-conceptual Knowledge of itself. It is the basis of all conceptual knowing. Consciousness is not perceivable, yet it is revealed through its objects, both gross and subtle.

The lustre of existence is Consciousness. The fundamental nature of existence is bliss (*Ananda*). *Shakti* and *Ananda* are inseparable lovers. What exists is Self-luminous Being-Consciousness. We are that. All else is a fairy tale; a story projected within the mind. Consciousness is its own foundation, i.e. Consciousness is the source of Beingness. In fact, it is Beingness.

Consciousness is Self-existent: there is nothing that precedes it, nothing that follows it, and nothing that it depends on. The subject/object duality is empirical consciousness, while no subject/no object is non-dual, pure Consciousness. Pure Consciousness is the substratum of empirical consciousness. There is always Consciousness, including consciousness of insentience. However, insentience is always inferred, never proven. Even a rock may be imbued in some sense with Consciousness. The most subtle is the most pervasive. What can be more subtle and therefore more pervasive than ether (space)? Pure Consciousness transcends even the extremely subtle ether; it transcends all of the polarities.

Consciousness simply is; it is not a thing, idea or a substance.

Therefore, to speak of an 'expansion' of Consciousness must mean that the range, depth or subtlety of perception and understanding is increasing, not Consciousness itself. Consciousness, being limitless, neither expands nor contracts. Consciousness always remains exactly what it is.

Awareness

> *'He who is not aware of the Self is an animal subject to creation, preservation and destruction...'*
> —*Atma Sakshatkara*, the Agamas

Consciousness knows itself as Awareness. Awareness is a manifestation of the illuminating Power of Consciousness.

The terms, Consciousness and Awareness, are like the two sides of a coin—on one side, there is pure Consciousness, which is empty of content (Consciousness-by-itself), i.e. transcendental, while on the other side is Awareness, which is Consciousness with content ('consciousness of...'), i.e. phenomenal. They appear to be different, but in fact are One and the same. Our true nature is called the Self because it is luminously and indivisibly Self-aware. The Self is neither more nor less than pure Consciousness. The Vedas state, 'Thou art That.'

When we see our thoughts or feel our feelings, we are seeing and feeling 'things', albeit, subtle things. Whatever we are 'conscious of...', whether subtle or gross, has its being in Consciousness, yet what we are 'conscious of...' is not the same thing as its substratum, Consciousness. What we are 'conscious of...' is not exactly real and not exactly unreal, because this awareness never fully reveals the exact nature of 'that' of which we are aware.

Sentience

Two rocks smashing against and destroying each other is not

considered vicious. Why? Because we believe that rocks are not sentient. If the rocks were conscious, then the act would be considered vicious. Consciousness, which is the source of sentience, always remains neutral and transcendent, analogous to the heat and light of the Sun that can both nourish and destroy the crops that feed us.

All thought of insentient matter, all observation however macrocosmic or microscopic, all theory, all evidence demands Consciousness. We can never get outside of Consciousness in order to verify the existence of the non-conscious. We may infer it, but we cannot prove it. Insentience cannot be proven.

11

PHILOSOPHY

'Always the beautiful answer who asks a more beautiful question.'

—E.E. Cummings (1894–1962)

Philosophy is always the means, never an end. When the oracle of Delphi was asked, 'Who is the wisest man in the world?', she answered, 'Socrates of Athens.' When Socrates heard this, his response was, 'Yes, I am the wisest man. Why? Because everyone thinks that they "know", but I "know" that "I do not know". That makes me the wisest man.'"

Philosophy decides neither for nor against the existence of God. It remains indifferent.

—Martin Heiddeger (1889–1976)

I suspect that Heidegger's flirtation with Nazism and its catastrophic consequences was the beginning of his real awakening to Being. Respect him or reject him, as a philosopher and ontologist, Martin Heidegger was a genius.

The great twentieth century Western philosophers such as Bertrand Russell, Martin Heidegger, Jean-Paul Sartre, etc. have demonstrated little desire to learn from India's Sages. There have been but a few exceptions, notably the nineteenth century philosopher Arthur Schopenhauer (1788–1860). In science, a great exception has been the Nobel Laureate Erwin Schrodinger (1887–1961) who drew many of his insights into quantum physics from India's ancient Vedic texts, specifically the Upanishads.

Other pioneers in quantum physics who have drawn inspiration from the Vedas include Niels Bohr, Albert Einstein, Werner Heisenberg, Robert Oppenheimer and Nikola Tesla. Eurocentrism has been the great weakness of the West and a cause of much suffering and abuse in foreign lands.

The value of philosophy is that it undermines dogmatism and fanaticism, two evils which promote intolerance and violence. For the Sages however, philosophy is largely irrelevant, although many, most notably Adi Shankara (8th century), have demonstrated brilliant analytic ability combined with their direct experience of the Self.

In his meditations, if René Descartes had been able to reach the state of 'no-thought' and perfect silent Self-awareness, instead of writing, 'I think, therefore I am', he would have written, 'I am, therefore I think'.

Thing-ness and Something-ness

Whatever is a 'thing' is by definition 'discrete'. Discreteness, i.e. distinct, separate objects and events, is a function of the limitations of our senses. Discreteness is only apparent; it is not real. There is neither something nor nothing 'exterior' to Consciousness. Whatever exists inheres in Consciousness. Any idea that something exists exterior to Consciousness is purely theoretical and unprovable. The same applies to the notion of interiority; there is nothing 'inside' of Consciousness.

Consciousness is not a 'thing' with an outside and an inside. However, for practical purposes, we may choose to assume an external world. Such an unprovable pragmatic assumption is legitimate for heuristic* reasons. 'Thing-ness' hides 'Something-ness' and 'Something-ness' hides 'Thing-ness', the two do not coexist; that is, they are not simultaneously apparent, though they are both there. 'Something-ness' is an incoherent mass of impressions that have not yet been defined as either discrete 'qualities' (e.g. blue, green, hot, cold), or discrete 'objects' (e.g. teapot, hammer) or discrete 'events' (e.g. falling, breaking). It is the intellect combined with memory that turns 'Something-ness' into 'Thing- ness'.

Thus, the intellect makes order out of the jumble of impressions that have been presented in Consciousness via the five senses and creates a description of an object, e.g. 'a teapot', or an event, e.g. 'a meeting'. Discrete objects and events are purely a creation of the mind. Coherence and incoherence cannot coexist simultaneously, hence there is either 'Thing-ness' or 'Something-ness', but never both at the same moment. For example, when we focus on the outline of a vase, we lose focus of the detailed image painted on its surface.

Alternatively, when we focus on the detailed image, we lose focus of the outline of the vase. 'Something-ness' demands a non-local 'witness', i.e. Consciousness, whereas 'Thing-ness' demands a local 'Seer', i.e. a subject in a body observing a 'thing' exterior to it.

'Something-ness' is primary; 'Thing-ness' is secondary and derivative. Don't go crazy with this, move on. Here is the question that can never by answered, 'Why is there "Something-ness" rather than absolute nothingness?' It is the same question as, 'Why is there Existence?', 'Why is there God?' and 'Why is there Consciousness?'. These 'whys' cannot be explained.

---

*'Heuristic' (def.): serving as an aid to learning, discovery, or problem-solving by experimental and trial-and-error methods.

As newborn babies, we quickly forget our Beingness and become obsessively hypnotized by 'Thing-ness'. We become narrowly focused; we long for 'things'. The result is that we become addicted to possessing and, in turn, we become possessed by our possessions. This leads to greed, competition, war and destruction. Who and what is the 'I' that possesses? In reality, no one possesses anything, not even their own body.

Phenomena (The Revealed) and Noumena (The Hidden)

> *'What can be said at all can be said clearly, and what we cannot talk about we must pass over in silence.'*
> —Ludwig Wittgenstein (1889–1951)

> *'We men know very little 'a priori', and have our senses to thank for nearly all our knowledge. Through experience we know only appearances..., but not the 'modum noumenon' (things as they are in themselves). God knows all things as they are in themselves, 'a priori' and immediately through an intuitive understanding....'*
> —Immanuel Kant (1724–1804)

> *'The best laid schemes o'mice an' men gang aft a-gley.'**
> —Robert Burns (1759–1796)

Pure Consciousness transcends empirical consciousness and permeates both the revealed (phenomena) and the hidden (noumena). Our senses limit us to the revealed (appearances). However, we have another, non-sensuous power called 'intuition'. We are too easily convinced by the phenomenal and we are profoundly mystified by the noumenal. We cannot be truly certain there is a noumenal—its existence is inferred from the phenomenal.

---

*Meaning: 'Whether a man or a mouse, the best plans are often disrupted by unknown forces.'

The undying, unbounded Self is the essence of both phenomenal and noumenal existence. When a man is motionless, we say he is not moving, even though within his body, billions of transactions are taking place. Simultaneously, with these internal transactions, the man is also standing on a small, rotating planet that is in constant revolution around the Sun. In the phenomenal world, there is no such thing as motionlessness.

Consciousness does not always involve perception; it is possible to 'be conscious', but without 'consciousness of…' anything (as at the moment of waking from sleep). However, the moment of perception itself involves consciousness and is always only a partial disclosure. Consciousness includes 'hiddenness' as well as 'appearance'. Consciousness includes 'awareness' of the possibility of hiddenness. Consciousness also includes awareness of 'revelation'; of 'that' which is revealed. Consciousness is the Being of both the hidden and the revealed.

Both hiddenness and revelation are always 'Here' and 'Now'. The essential nature of time is hidden (noumenal). Time revealed is a creation of the mind and unreal. There is only now.

There are no phenomena outside of Consciousness. Phenomena presuppose Consciousness. The phenomenal manifestation, i.e. that which is revealed, no matter how limited or distorted, influences the actions of sentient creatures, which in turn affects the noumenal, i.e. that which is hidden. Equally, the hidden influences the revealed. In fact, simply a belief in the hidden influences the revealed. This is why we often justify our unexpectedly bad behaviour by saying, 'The Devil made me do it.' Of course, what has just been written is inferred, not proven. However, the inference is a strong one.

There is an objective-correlative* (the hidden) to the contents

---

*'Objective-correlative' (def.): We assume that there is a hidden 'correlative' to whatever 'object' we see. We believe we see only a surface and that something hidden lies behind it. This is an assumption, not a given.

of consciousness (the revealed), but more than that, we cannot say. The vibration arising in Consciousness, that is to say, 'perception' is somehow linked to the hidden objective-correlative. That link is a creation of the power of Consciousness (*Chit-Shakti*).

The true nature of the objective-correlative, i.e. the unseen side of the universe, must be infinite and partless. The attribution of finiteness and discreteness to 'supposed' undisclosed objects and events is an unreal creation of the mind—an assumption superimposed upon an unseen, unprovable objective-correlative.

Ultimately, all phenomena are unreal, being merely appearances superimposed upon the substratum of Consciousness. The source of the apparent physical universe itself transcends physicality and, in fact, transcends all polarities; it is also called the Supreme Being or *Shiva* (God). Scientific enquiry is an empirical investigation into the nature of the noumenal (hidden) via the phenomenal (disclosed).

Hence, there is the endless and arduous process of trial and error that never arrives at 'absolute' proof. The disclosed is disclosed to the mind, as the hidden is hidden to the mind. The hidden, however, is not hidden to Being. Nor is the disclosed, disclosed to Being. For the man of Knowledge, i.e. the Sage, there is no 'this side' or 'that side', only limitless Being-Consciousness. Notions of 'hidden' and 'disclosed' pertain only to mind.

The noumenal, as assumed by sense-data is not identical with the sense-data, just as a tree captured in a photograph is not identical with the tree. In fact, there is a vast difference; a gulf that cannot be crossed. It is called 'inference'. The 'thing-in-itself' (noumenon) cannot be precisely talked about except to say that it is the material ground of the appearance. We can never know the ground directly although it is generally assumed to be energy/matter. We can surmise that the nature of the ground is an interplay of energies. These energies create the flows and tensions which give rise to the appearances of form, weight, solidity, fluidity, colour, sound, etc.

Whatever is hidden is what is not perceived, yet supposedly exists. What is disclosed is what is perceived and exists only as an appearance. The hidden and the disclosed are like two sides of a coin—only one side is perceived, yet the other side supposedly exists. Flip the coin around and the side that was hidden now becomes disclosed as an appearance, while the side that was disclosed now becomes hidden. The existence of both sides, however, is not in question 'if' we hold that physical reality is more than appearance alone. This is the big 'if' that very few are willing to question.

The term, 'universe' includes all that is hidden and all that is disclosed. The 'hidden', however, is always an assumption, whereas the 'disclosed' is direct experience. All inferred objects may or may not exist. In other words, the existence of an objective reality independent of Consciousness is a possibility, but not a given. Proving the possibility that something exists independent of Consciousness is impossible since the very process of proving itself involves Consciousness.

Whatever the big, hidden 'It' is that we are playing with, it does not, in any way, resemble the perceptions that make up the world of our direct experience. Therefore, humanity should be careful and not easily persuaded, while scientists and those financing them should be extremely cautious in the application of their findings. Unfortunately, political and financial interests frequently take priority over the basic rights and needs of humanity and the environment.

Relativity and the Absolute

That which is relative is only 'apparently' real. The real is absolute, transcending all relativity, yet functions as the substratum of the dream of relativity.

Projection

The world is our projection. We create our own description of it, but our description often fails to stand up. As a result, we live with anxiety. All of this is the projection of our own mind. We should call our projection into question, but unfortunately most of us never do. We buy into the story that we ourselves have created. We have the option to abandon it.

We can 'tear ourselves away'—to paraphrase Sartre—from our story when we enquire, 'For whom is this thought of the world?' When we look for the 'I', who is the source of this thought? We cannot find it because the 'I' cannot turn and see itself. In the attempt, the 'I' simply disappears and what remains is a moment of absolute Silence and contentless Self-awareness. For a brief flash, both the subject and the object are no more. This is the beginning of awakening and it is called 'Self-enquiry'. When there is no ego/subject and no world/object, what remains is the state of pure Being-Consciousness.

The Senses

All that is ever experienced via the senses is a relative universe, which is no proof that the universe is actually relative. The five senses rule the majority of people, keeping them in ignorance of the Self. The limited consciousness of our mind is a mere reflection of Self-Consciousness. Our limited consciousness is a blanket of ignorance, yet we must respect it for pragmatic reasons. There is 'seeing house', 'hearing noise', but there is no 'seeing a house', 'hearing a noise', because there is no one to see, and no one to hear. There is only 'seeing house' and 'hearing noise' appearing within the Self.

Sense is not sense unless there is sensing, and there is no sensing in the absence of Consciousness. Without the senses, there is no empirical mind. The mind feeds on sense-experience. Pure mind is Self-Awareness without an object. The apparatus of perceiving, i.e. the senses, simultaneously gives and limits knowledge. Limited knowledge produces a thirst for greater knowledge, at least for some, and that leads to the gradual evolution towards Self-realization.

Sense-data and Qualities

Out of meaningless 'impressions', a meaningful world is created. This world is a mental act which involves Consciousness. Meaningless impressions are neither mental nor material; they simply are. They too have their being in Consciousness. The data of the senses, i.e. impressions, are simply undefined appearances appearing in Consciousness; no volition is required. Volition is required to give both definition and a name to those appearances, and this action makes them a mental entity.

'Qualities', here, refer to impressions, i.e. 'sense-data', such as colour, sound or shape, but not to objects. Objects are configured from a variety of qualities, for example, a 'blue', 'pear-shaped', 'solid' object, e.g. a vase. Qualities, even though they have no real existence, presuppose existence. Their appearance, even if it is only for a fraction of a second, proves existence.

The Universe

A universe that is void of Consciousness is a meaningless universe and is no different than a non-existent universe. The very notion of an unconscious universe of which we sentient creatures are an integral part is absurd. The universe is fundamentally organic, just as the human body is organic. It has a definite integrity, is governed by intelligence and is pervaded by Consciousness. The physical universe is not independent of Consciousness, rather it has its being in Consciousness.

This universe, which appears substantial, is in fact insubstantial. For instance, the hands feel solidity where in truth there is none. The universe is an apparition of both equilibrium and disequilibrium; however, there is neither equilibrium nor disequilibrium in reality. The universe is formless, appearing as form and then dissolving, all the while remaining formless—it is a magic show.

Creation

The creation of the universe is from the fine to the dense; its dissolution will be from the dense to the fine. Creation neither increases nor decreases the transcendental Self. Mass must always have its exact polarity, bringing it back to zero. The human 'cause and effect' mind cannot conceive of an uncreated Source of creation. Yet it must be so! Timeless uncaused Consciousness is the source.

Duality and Difference

Regard the perceiver and the perceived as the Self—there is no real duality. When perception is seen as it truly is, i.e. Consciousness, all duality and 'otherness' disappears. The perceiver, the perceived and the perceiving are an identity. True direct perception is only being it. Discreteness, whether phenomenal or otherwise, really does exist, but as an illusion.

Difference is not a sensuous intuition; it is a mental determination, an interpretation that is required for our description of the world. Non-duality includes duality and does not stand in opposition to it. All apparent dualism is sublated by non-duality. Since the Self is partless, it can only 'apparently' become many, but not actually. Thus, multiplicity is merely an appearance—it is not reality.

The wave within the water is simply fluctuation and movement, it has no independent existence. There is no such 'thing' as a wave. The wave is not different from the water and therefore has no relationship with water, only with the other waves. The apparent duality of different waves is sublated by the singular reality of water. We can infer an external world but we can never prove it, since we cannot escape the very Consciousness in which the world appears. Thus, a world that is external to Consciousness is neither proven nor disproven. This leaves us—in our waking state—in a perpetual existential doubt about its reality or unreality.

There is, of course, a world that is external to our physical body, but our body is also appearing in Consciousness and so its existence externally to its appearance remains in question. We are left with the same doubt, 'Does this body of mine exist externally to its appearance in (my) Consciousness or is it merely a "dream body"?' What we can be certain of is this—our bodies, our thoughts, our feelings and emotions, our friendships and other relationships, our home, our work, our world, etc. do exist, but in Consciousness; thus, our self-identity exists in Consciousness. In short, whatever we know or experience exists in Consciousness, unequivocally. This understanding is not to deny the possibility of a world, etc. which is independent of Consciousness. And we are free to act—in fact, must *act*—as if there is a world that is independent, but we must hold this position tentatively, not dogmatically.

Alternatively, whatever appears in Consciousness cannot be denied. All appearances are real, even those appearances which turn out to be illusions, such as a mirage of water in a parched desert. An appearance is an appearance and it cannot be denied; it is real as an appearance—just as a movie is real as a movie, even though the content is fantasy. It is the content of appearances that is relative, changing and subject to doubt. The Consciousness in which appearances occur, however, is the unchanging substratum of all appearance and persists throughout the three states of waking, dreaming and sleeping.

Cause and Effect

'...the end precedes the beginning,
And the end and the beginning were always there
Before the beginning and after the end.'
—*Burnt Norton*, T.S. Eliot (1888–1965)

'If the cause is produced from the effect and if the effect is again, produced from the cause, which of the two is born first upon which depends the birth of the other?'
—Gaudapada (8th century AD)

There is no such thing as a cause without an effect or an effect without a cause; they are an inseparable unit. Every effect becomes a cause; every cause becomes an effect. How can there possibly be a real, material first cause or final effect? In either case, there must be a before or an after, which leads to the absurdity of a beginningless infinite regression or its opposite.

Just as the sequence of events in a video can be sped up or slowed down, the same can be done with the world-appearance. Potentially, everything can occur at once, in which case there is no such thing as cause and effect. As soon as time comes into play, so does the impression of sequence. This impression creates the idea of cause and effect. Whatever precedes the present moment is termed 'cause' and whatever follows the present moment is termed 'effect'. The present moment itself, i.e. the now, is both cause and effect, and they cancel each other. Since the present moment is the only moment that ever 'is', cause and effect are unreal.

The ultimate source of the universe is itself uncaused. It must be, otherwise there is the impossible scenario of an infinite regression. Being uncaused, there is no real effect, cause or time. Cause can never be separated from effect, nor can effect be separated from cause. Every cause is itself an effect. Truly, there can be neither a first cause nor a first effect. Like logic and mathematics, cause and effect are creations of the mind and serve its purposes.

In the mind-created framework of time, an effect can persist only as long as it is sustained by its causative force, thus a finite cause can never produce an infinite effect. A cause is effect, an effect is cause—they are two sides of the same coin. There is no duality, no beginning and no end in timeless reality.

'Cause and effect' must be understood as a heuristic, not absolute principle. What is called 'effect' is inherent in what we call 'cause'. Ultimately, there is no real cause or effect, just like there is no time sequence of seconds, minutes and hours. Material cause is some form of energy that has a relative equipoise (stasis); whereas efficient cause is energy in a dynamic (non-static) state. 'Efficient' and 'material' are merely relative terms. There is no absolute distinction between them.

Cause and effect are simply ways of describing energy (cause) and form (effect). All we ever 'see' is effect (form). Kinetic energy is never without form, however subtle, and form is never absolutely static. Science studies effect and tries to work its way back to the original cause. The effect is non-different from the cause. The effect is appearance, the cause alone is real. Both the real and the appearance have their being in the Self. Cause is never revealed, only its effect; substance is never revealed, only its qualities; power is never revealed, only its manifestation. This is the basis of scientific enquiry.

Effect may exist in the form of pure potentiality (*Shakti*) before it manifests as first cause, but this primal form will be impossible to see or analyze. If there is cause then appearance is always effect. By extension, our bodies, actions, thoughts, feelings and emotions are caused appearances and merely effects. Who are we then? An effect? Impossible! We are that to which the appearance is revealed in the eternal now. The Supreme Being is both the material and efficient uncaused cause. We are the Self who witnesses its effects and who is also not different from it. God has no employees.

Time and Space

> *'Time past and time future*
> *What might have been and what has been*
> *Point to one end, which is always present.'*
> —Burnt Norton, T.S. Eliot (1888–1965)

> *'Time no longer appears to us as a gigantic, world-dominating chronos, nor as a primitive entity, but as something derived from phenomena themselves. It is a figment of my thinking.'*
> —Erwin Schrödinger (1887–1961)

Every human being adopts a few universally held, apparently reasonable assumptions about the nature of things. They are:

1. That we inhabit a vast universe.
2. That this universe is composed of matter and energy.
3. That there is such a thing as space.
4. That there is such a thing as time.
5. That some sort of event must have occurred to cause this universe of energy, matter, space and time.

At first glance, all of the above appear self-evident and empirically sound. Why should we question what our five senses so clearly present? However, while the first four assumptions are, for practical purposes, almost impossible to discount, the fifth raises a serious challenge.

Physics indicates that our particular universe had a definite beginning and will probably have a definite end. Of course, our universe may be only one of many universes and if so, then the totality of all universes, i.e. 'The Universe', may well have had a starting point. If so, there must have been an event that started it all. Whatever the exact nature of this primal event, we must assign to it the status of 'first cause'. This raises the question, 'How did the first cause come into being?' Some 'thing' cannot arise out of absolute nothingness.

Every cause must itself be the effect of a preceding cause. We all assume cause and effect because we witness successions of events and a forward moving causal connection between those events. Or at least, we believe we do. We cannot conceive of an effect without a cause and at the same time, we cannot conceive of a cause that is not itself the effect of a previous cause. And so, from our standpoint as human beings, there can be no empirical first cause and The Universe must be beginningless. That as it may be, can causality and time really exist?

The difference between the manifest and the unmanifest is absolute; there is no causal relation. It is equivalent to the absolute difference between 0 and 1 (nothing and something), as opposed to the relative difference between 1 and 2 (something and something). In reality, there is no first cause, but there is the principle of potentiality. Potentiality is not nothingness, as in the case of '0'. Potentiality is power that has yet to manifest as kinetic energy. This is consistent with the understanding of potential and kinetic energy in physics. What would have preceded the 'Big Bang' cannot be nothingness; what preceded this primal event was and is beginningless *Shakti*.

Physical space (*akasha*) is a more subtle substance than air, air is more subtle than water, water is more subtle than earth. At the end of 'time', space, air, water and earth recede into the source from which they emerged, only to re-emerge in a new cycle. But whether they withdraw or emerge, they never leave their source, which is *Shiva* (God)/*Shakti* (Power). This is the view of *advaita* Vedanta, which is the pinnacle of Vedic wisdom. As for the poetic beginning and end of time, empirical time is sublated by timelessness. There is no duality between source (*Shiva/Shakti*) and Creation (the Universe)—they are One, there is no second. The truth is, nothing ever happens, not really.

The beginning implies time. What beginning? What time? Who invented time? Does time exist independently of the mind? Beyond mind, there is no time; rather, we superimpose the impression of time on timeless reality. We created time to manage our 'doingness'. Beyond this, time is meaningless.

Time is only relative to the play of objectivity, as are the notions of beginning and end. If there is no finest particle—and it is obvious that there is no finest, material particle—then the idea of objectivity becomes meaningless, as does the idea of beginning and end, i.e. time.

Just as time is relative, so is space. Remove all phenomena and you remove the impression of space—you cancel space itself. Remove time and space, and limitless existence remains, as does limitless Consciousness. Being is a 'no-thing' that can never be obliterated—it is not nothingness. Materialists may not agree with this. Our notion of time and space is a creation of our mind; our mind, a creation of *Shakti* (power); and *Shaki*, an inherent principle of absolute Consciousness (*Paramatman*).

This vibrant pulsation emanating from *Shakti* as *prana* is the cause of time and space, objects and events. The Supreme Self (*Paramatman*) is not affected by this pulsation, since it is the very source of this pulsation of expansion and contraction, appearing and disappearing, movement and stillness.

The impressions of time and space are a function of the vibrating power of *Shakti*. *Shakti* and its manifestations have their Being in Consciousness, the ultimate source, the Supreme Being. To the mind, there appears to be time (sequence) and space (dimension), however, the sense of sequence and dimension is actually a projection of the mind—a projection that never leaves the mind. Reality includes the impression of cause, effect, time and space, but these impressions—occurring in the mind—have no reality exterior to the mind.

The illusion of time creates the illusion of space; the illusion of space reinforces the illusion of time, and vice versa. It's a merry-go-round. Pure space (*akasha*) is not empty, it is full. Full with what? It is full to the brim with power, i.e. energy and vital force. It has neither dimension nor duration and is extremely subtle.

Our ordinary human concepts pertaining to measurement do not apply to these ontological realities.

All relativities have their being in Consciousness yet Consciousness is not touched by them, remaining in its unmanifested state of pure potential and seeming not to exist. The Power inherent in Consciousness manifests but never leaves its transcendent source. There never was a time when this was not. There is no such thing as a beginning. There will be no such thing as an ending. Human beginnings and endings are merely relative markers. Timelessness is not boring; to be bored is to be caught in time. Therefore, let us end the boogeyman of time.

Free Will and Determinism

> *'Shape without form, shade without colour, Paralysed force, gesture without motion...'*
> —*The Hollow Men*, T.S. Eliot (1888–1965)

> *'...men believe themselves to be free...because they are conscious of their actions...'*
> —Baruch Spinoza (1632–1677)

> *'The history of the world is none other than the process of the consciousness of freedom.'*
> —Georg Wilhelm Friedrich Hegel (1770–1831)

This sense of freedom is illusory. Since choice always happens in the present moment, it appears 'as if' we have free will. This appearance is based on an illusion. The choice that we believe we make freely has already been determined by the totality of cosmic momentum unfolding in the eternal Here and Now. The twin notions of fate and free will are a product of the egoic mind and pertain only to the body-mind. They don't even apply to the Self. It is our ignorance that imprisons us in this false duality. Thus, the Sage affirms, 'All is God's doing.'

Predestination is not determined from without; it is determined from within by one's inherent motivation to seek happiness. Ignorance will have us look for happiness in wrong places, but the inner drive to experience felicity will inevitably push us to keep looking, exploring, and seeking. In this way, gradually we overcome our ignorance and discover the truth of ourselves and our oneness with the Supreme Being.

Self-effort is more powerful than planetary influences. However, we must develop our personal power. Personal power implies the confidence and courage to make our own choices and to be true to ourselves. But this is not the whole truth…

We are not prisoners of predestination, but neither are we solitary unaccountable free agents. Thus, the notion that goals are 'freely chosen' is a fallacy. This apparent paradox is the result of a wrong assumption of a duality of self and Self. In reality, no such duality exists, since the egoic self is an illusory creation of the mind. The true Self exists, while the egoic self is bogus. Thus, our authentic 'free will' is God's doing and 'God's doing' is our free will. The Self that we are is not different from the Supreme Being, and we cannot compete with that Being which we already are. Our suffering is born of our ignorance of our true nature.

The doctrine of duality is the Achilles heel of the Abrahamic western religions and has created a kind of schizophrenic self-contradictory thought process in which we find ourselves constantly at war with ourselves. In reality, there is no such thing as duality, but one cannot overcome the illusion of duality through logic and analysis alone. Duality is overcome by the direct experience of non-duality, i.e. Oneness, Wholeness.

'Free will' means simply that we, and no other, are fully responsible for our choices and actions, but not as autonomous actors who are separate from the source. Paradoxically, all of our choices have already been determined for us by our past actions and experience, but we are not sufficiently clairvoyant to recognize how and why.

If you are watching a movie that grips your attention, your mind, emotions and even physical postures will get caught up in the forces that are working themselves out on the screen. If you voluntarily choose to shift your attention away from the contents of the movie and onto the screen itself, then all these cinematic forces and your reactions to them will disappear. You always have the freedom to shift your attention this way, but whether you will or will not is already predetermined—this is the paradox of free will and determinism!

Those who are true seekers learn how to shift their attention away from the world-movie and onto the supporting screen, i.e. the substratum of pure Consciousness. All inner progress is a function of intention, but the desire for progress must already exist. Sadly, most of the inhabitants of this planet lack this desire and, by default, remain on the wheel of *karma* (repetitive existence).

Your freedom of choice to re-focus your attention to and from the screen itself is, in fact, predetermined. Even the thought, 'I have free will', has been pre-determined. Individual freedom of choice is sublated by Supreme intent. Whatever choice we make has been influenced by our past—a past which we have largely forgotten. For this reason, the impression is created that our choices are freely made.

In truth, however, our choices are determined by past experience. It must not be forgotten that every thought and every action will have its own consequences—consequences for which we will be fully responsible. To the limited mind, all this is an inexplicable paradox. In Yoga philosophy, however, this is called *karma*, i.e. the sum of our past actions bringing inevitable results upon us. We should not arrogantly assume that someone's personal tragedy is a result of evil past actions. No one is qualified to make such a judgement.

Choices which we have allowed others to choose for us are not authentically our own, they are inauthentic. Nevertheless, we are responsible for having allowed it. We had the freedom to say 'No'. Or did we? It comes to this—the Self is free. We are not different from the Self, therefore, we too are free. It is our ignorance and our unexamined assumption that who we are is the body-mind, and it traps us in the dilemma, 'Are we free or not?' Again, it comes to this—the body-mind is not free, it is insentient, while who we are is the sentient Self.

The problem is that we forgot who we are. We wrongly believe we are creatures moving about on Earth, and we mistakenly assume that we are the sentient, small self of the body-mind. Because we have forgotten our true nature, we find ourselves on the horns of a dilemma. This dilemma clouds our thinking and our actions. When we awaken to the Self, the dilemma evaporates, like the early morning mist at sunrise. We are free; we were always free; it's just that we forgot.

If we are not different from the Supreme Being; if the idea that we are separate is an illusion; if, in fact, there is no real duality, then the notions of free will and determinism become meaningless and the whole idea of these opposing possibilities is nullified. If we awaken to the Self, which is not different from the Supreme Being, then gone is our delusion that somehow we are in control or that somehow something greater than ourselves is controlling us. We realize that everything is simply 'happening' and there is no real 'cause and effect'. Gone is the idea that we are the 'effect' of something other than ourselves or the 'cause' that shapes the destiny of another person. We discover that we are merely witnessing an awe-inspiring play of images, sounds and sensations unfolding within a unified field of limitless Being-Consciousness.

Now and Here

However far we may travel, we are always exactly where we are. Here is never far and far is never here. What is known is what is present; what is present is what is known. That which is not present may be known conceptually. In such a case, it is a concept that is known in the present, and not the 'thing' the concept refers to. Everything is happening now. Events merely appear to be sequential.

If there was such a thing as the Big Bang, when did it happen? It happened now. It will also finish now. We were born now and we will also die now. All cause and all effect is happening now. 'Now! Now!' said the materialist in wonder and the empiricist in disbelief when they heard the Sage speak thus.

Experience

> '...the real table, if there is one, is not the same as what we immediately experience by sight or touch or hearing. The real table, if there is one, is not 'immediately' known to us at all, but must be an 'inference' from what is immediately known.'
> —Bertrand Russell (1872–1970)

Only through direct experience will we discover what can be of real use to us. By 'Experience' (*capital 'E'*), which means 'Realization' of the true Self, we realize that the world is merely a stream of thought-forms. Then, it ceases to imprison us. Direct Experience of the Self itself washes away all impurities and delusions of the mind. Direct Experience is always present; our only obstacle is the obscuring veil of conceptual knowledge and unexamined assumptions.

All we have as a subject is our objective experience, and from this experience, the intellect infers a universe. We then analyze and explore the universe that our intellect has inferred, and we test the validity of our analyses, assumptions, etc. to verify if our conclusions are correct. Our conclusions concerning the inferred universe can never be absolutely certain because we have no way of proving beyond any shadow of doubt that our inferred universe actually exists independently of our subjective experience of it. This is the problem!

Philosophers and scientists have argued from the beginning—if, indeed, there was a beginning—about the first cause, the nature of time and space, the conflict of fate versus free will, etc., however, there have been no settled conclusions, nor will there ever be. The Sage teaches that there can be no final conclusions unless and until the true Self is realized. Answers to these difficult questions will be revealed only through direct Experience and not through the false, limiting screen of subject/ object duality. Experience itself is the experiencer. There is no separate experiencer who experiences, nor are there any two experiences which are identical.

My experience of another describing his experience is simply my experience. It is not possible to escape my experience. The Self can be obscured but never abandoned. It is all there is. Experience in not happening to the Self, it is simply revealed within and by virtue of the Self. There is no duality; all apparent duality is unreal. Experience in itself is not unreal, but what ordinary experience refers to or suggests may be unreal.

All thought, as thought, is directly experienced. Direct Experience is the immediate apprehension of that which precedes reflection. Reflection is thinking about that which has been experienced directly. 'Thinking about' is always conceptional.

Conceptual meaning is also a function of reflection, yet it is second-hand. Direct Experience includes the process of reflection, yet reflection itself is secondary to direct experience. People often confuse their direct Experience of something with their reflection on that experience. Every conceptual or reflective thought is itself a direct Experience, even though what the thought refers to is not.

All direct Experience is immediate, whereas whatever is referred to is merely inferential, i.e. second-hand knowledge. The big hidden 'it' that we are struggling to understand does not in any way resemble the perceptions which make up the world of our direct experience. Our direct Experience does not reveal what is hidden, only what is disclosed. Therefore, humanity should be cautious. Whatever is experienced, i.e. perceived, thought, felt, speculated, assumed, questioned, deduced, etc. is 'knowledge', but with a small 'k'.

The totality of Experience has its being in the Self, but the Self is not limited to any specific content of experience, such as the body or feelings or thoughts, or even the totality of experience itself. We are so mesmerized by objective experience that we have amnesia with regard to the very foundation of experience, which is Consciousness itself.

Intent and Intentionality

Personal power implies the confidence and courage to make our own choices, to be true to our Self and to let go of the ego. It also implies strong intentionality. Intentionality is a manifestation of the Power (*Shakti*) inherent in pure Consciousness. Pure Consciousness is not intentional and it remains in its pure state as Self-Consciousness. This Consciousness has no object, nor does it have a subject. It transcends all polarities. Self-Consciousness, in fact, permeates intentional consciousness, much as a movie screen permeates the film being played on its surface.

By analogy, just as the screen is forgotten while attention is focused on the objects and events projected onto it, the Self-Consciousness is forgotten when *Shakti* assumes the form of intentionality. Just as when the movie is over, what remains is what was always there as the substratum or ground, i.e. the screen itself, when the intentional consciousness fades what remains is the eternal substratum, Self-Consciousness. Intentional consciousness always has its subject and object, whereas Self-Consciousness has no object and no subject, abiding forever in its own Beingness.

Intention is always and only occurring now. The realization of a vision or objective does not happen in time, rather it is something that is unfolding always in the present. Intention is felt only in the present. The built-in desire to see, hear, learn, etc. produces the organs of eyes, ears, brain, etc. In other words, the body and its organs develop as a function of sentience and intention, not accident.

Intention presupposes an object of consciousness, thus intentional consciousness is always 'consciousness-of-something'. The mind's formation of an object of consciousness from a mass of sense-data also presupposes intention. Intentionality and objectivity—whether subtle or gross—are inseparable; one cannot exist without the other. Without intention, the object-world ('thing-ness') will not manifest in Consciousness, leaving only a mass of undefinable impressions (indeterminate 'something-ness').

Ultimately, goals and intentions arise from a universal, Supreme intent that inheres in the Absolute. Just as *prana* (vital force) is a manifestation of the Absolute's *Shakti* (power), intent—the governing principle of Creation—arises from the same potency. It is our delusions, arising from ignorance of our true nature, that give rise to objectives and means that are a distorted reflection of intent, leading to actions that are misguided, feeble and which result in suffering.

Our conquest of self-ignorance is ultimately a function of intent. Until we win this battle and awaken to our true nature, our ordinary human intentions will be based primarily on our polarized egoic desires and fears—we desire something appealing; we fear something unpleasant; our life is a roller coaster. The Sage lives from pure intent, not ordinary human intentionality. The intent of a Sage is extremely powerful and sheds Grace all around. Pure intent is the divine governing principle of all right action. Affirm, 'I choose the Power of pure intent.' Then, meditate on it.

Superimposition

A superimposition is a wrong notion about the reality underlying an appearance; it is misperceiving one thing for another. A superimposition is a false appearance, a mirage, just like when we see a distant pool of blue in the desert and wrongly believe that it is a body of water.

Here is another example of superimposition. A man says, 'I thought what I saw in the shadow was a snake and so I was afraid and ran, but it turned out to be only a piece of rope!' Here, the snake was a false superimposition on the actual rope; the snake was an illusion. These kinds of superimposition are common and easily understood.

A more subtle form of superimposition and one more difficult to detect, occurs when finite empirical space such as the space occupied by our physical body, is wrongly superimposed on the pure, limitless space of the Self. Most people are unaware that by this they are unconsciously accepting the illusion that the body and the Self are related. They are not. The space of the Self is pure Consciousness; it is non-dimensional, unlike finite, empirical space. The body does not 'take up space' in the Self. The body has its being in the Self, but the Self does not have its being in the body. Bodies come and go, are created and destroyed, while the timeless Self remains as it is.

After the death of the gross body, the subtle body continues. But this subtle body is also limited and has its being in the Self. To identify the subtle body as the Self is therefore also a false superimposition. The Self is neither the gross nor the subtle body; it both pervades and transcends all appearances and experience. The Self always remains in its true nature as Being-Consciousness. We are that.

We suffer in fear of death because the whole phenomenon of birth, change and death is falsely superimposed upon that which is birthless, changeless and deathless—the undying Self. The Self is never born and never dies. We inhabit the body but we are not the body; we are Being-Consciousness; we are the Self. When the Self is realized all fear of death and suffering evaporates.

Why? Because our fear is based on an illusion—the false belief that the Self and the body are the same thing. Not so. As the Self, we inhabit the body, but we are not the body—we are pure Consciousness; we are the Self that never dies.

Language

We use language to keep ourselves and others predictable and mired in the status quo. Our limited perception creates the illusions of solidity, immobility, materiality, discreteness and 'things-in-themselves'. These illusions are reinforced by language. Words refer, directly or indirectly, to something other than themselves. Their meaning is given to them by the intellect. Coherent collections of words are merely descriptions. Reflected Consciousness, which is the world-appearance, remains simply what It is—Consciousness.

That which is beyond all relativity cannot be defined as either empty or full. The Self transcends all of the polarities of language. All the multiplicity of words become resolved into one word— AUM (OM). All the images of vision become resolved into one vision—pure light. All of time and all of space become resolved into one omnipresence—Now and Here.

Logic

Logic is another form of language. The notions of true and false can apply, in a strict sense, only to the propositions of logic and mathematics, i.e. to abstractions. In our sensory world, it is more accurate to use general terms such as coherence/incoherence, harmony/disharmony, resonance/dissonance, reasonable/unreasonable, etc. Imposing the propositions of logic upon our sensory world serves only to create more, rather than less, meaningless and often dangerous assumptions. $2 + 2 = 4$ is a creation of the mind and does not exist in the sleep state.

The logical structure of language mirrors the logical structure of the world; conversely, the logical structure of the world mirrors the logical structure of language. Which came first, chicken or egg? The inductive verification of theories renders them always tentative, i.e. not false, but not even definitely true. Categories (of objects) are mental creations based on relative sense data; they are not hard facts or indubitable truths.

12

LEADERSHIP

The greatest leader is the Sage, that Illumined One, who has no history, no future and no agenda, and who leads not from saying or doing, but from Being. A Self-leader is neither a leader of the pack nor a follower of the herd. Leaders are seldom born; leadership must be gained through trial, error and dogged determination. Authentic leaders do not pull people about by the nose, rather they challenge people to assume full responsibility for whatever it is they are facing, and inspire them with the confidence that they are sufficient for the task.

The true leader may be well-acquainted with the transcendent, but he remains fully grounded in the here and now of the phenomenal world. For him, the dichotomy between Spirit and matter is unreal.

Action and Work

'Established in Being, perform action.'
—The Bhagavad Gita

All human beings are born for work that is naturally suited to them. The trick is to recognize what that work is. A wandering scattered mind will be best controlled by occupying it with something that is purposive and enjoyable. Therefore, the best work is work to which we are naturally suited. This is called *svadharma* (the path of one's own being). When the foundation for action is weak, things will slide toward an endless horizon of incompleteness. Entropy will set in. Practise sustained concentration daily to develop will.

Whatever is done with a clear, peaceful, non-egoic mind is right action; whatever is done from an agitated, self-serving mind is wrong action. Action is not a means to realize the Self. Action produces results and the Self is not a result, nor is the realization of the Self a result. Cause and effect have no relationship to the Self. Self-realization is a bestowal of Grace, earned after much earnest practice. One who identifies himself with unnecessary activity cannot be absorbed in the Self.

The path of right action leads to wisdom, while avoiding responsibility leads to delusion and destruction. The mind and senses are purified through a commitment to right action. Consciousness allows action; it does not do action. Stay conscious and alert. Caring is love in action, whereas careless, cold action kills life. Devotion empowers action. Contentment is not a synonym for resignation, which means quitting. One can be content in the present, even in the face of great difficulties, by holding to the original intention and persistently taking action to manifest it. If the intention is pure, Grace will ultimately prevail.

Doing is not being, but being is required for doing. Underneath the doingness is the beingness. Be the beingness first, then the doing will be the right action. Knowing and doing cannot be separated. Knowing involves doing; doing involves knowing. The Great Knowledge, however, transcends ordinary knowing and doing.

What truly moves us lies waiting just behind the conditioned mind that we wrongly believe is our self. Until we become familiar with our true nature, from where our real choices and actions are motivated, we will be frustrated in our efforts to live our potential and realize our dreams.

Communication

> 'We are the hollow men We are the stuffed men Leaning together Headpiece filled with straw. Alas! Our dried voices, when We whisper together Are quiet and meaningless...'
> —*The Hollow Men*, T.S. Eliot (1888–1965)

We must look beyond the literal meaning of words and gestures if we are to discover the true intention behind any communication. Communication that is empowering motivates people to take effective action for producing concrete and positive results. Transformational communication rides a wave of clear, strong intention, reflecting a high degree of Self-awareness.

Communicating for empowerment demands first a personal commitment to cleaning up our internal dialogue. The second step demands that we root out our unconscious negatives and burn them in the fire of Self-awareness.

Responsibility

Those who have assumed responsibility for their lives and demonstrate mastery in the field of action will inspire others to rise to their full potential as well. Responsibility begins with the recognition that we are not separate from the ultimate source of our own experience. The moment we choose to assume responsibility for both our personal history and our current situation, we will be able to opt for becoming an enlightened leader. Again, the moment one truly assumes responsibility for whatever was, is and will be, is the moment when one's life undergoes a profound transformation.

Each choice to assume responsibility for what is rightfully ours is an act of personal empowerment that strengthens the edifice of our self-esteem. Until we know ourselves, we cannot know our true responsibilities. In simple fact, our first responsibility is to know the Self. Once attained, we shall then see what other responsibilities there may be.

The philosopher Martin Heidegger wrote that authentic existence is a function of assuming absolute responsibility for where we find ourselves. How true! The Sage Ramana Maharshi said, 'Throw all of your burdens on the Supreme Being and be at peace.' How true! We can do both.

13

SOCIETY

'This is the dead land This is cactus land Here the stone images
Are raised, here they receive
The supplication of a dead man's hand
Under the twinkle of a fading star.'
—The Hollow Men, T.S. Eliot (1888–1965)

'From our human experience and history, at least as far as I am informed, I know that everything essential and great has only emerged when human beings had a home and were rooted in a tradition.'
—Martin Heidegger (1889–1976)

'Nothing is more surprising than the easiness with which the many are governed by the few.'
—David Hume (1711–1776)

The egoic mind is an oppressor, and until it is conquered, there will be neither justice nor peace in this world. If one stands up for the truth, one will be attacked. History proves this.

In the beginning, I was interested in economics. I wanted to make a difference, but the professors of economics with their models, statistics and theories, killed my interest, so I turned to philosophy and ontology. Then, I discovered the Upanishads and the Vedanta. Today, I appreciate all of it. Material poverty is, ultimately, a manifestation of spiritual poverty, and so we resort to manipulation, lies, theft and violence to have our needs met.

Wealth accumulated through self-effort is good. However, we must be cautious. The money rolled out in sheets and metal coins is *Maya* (illusion), it is unreal, it is a mind game. This mind game, used to manipulate the distribution of wealth in favour of those who know how to play the game, is starving the poor, corrupting the wealthy and turning the dispossessed into criminals. This money-game of money-men is the creation of a powerful egoic mind. It kills the environment and destroys the very foundation upon which all life depends for survival. It is demonic.

Technology is not Knowledge, it will never set us free. Technological know-how is limited empirical knowledge and is not capable of saving us from ourselves or from the forces surrounding us. Its sheer blind power has taken humanity to the brink. Only the Great Knowledge can transform our current situation. Until we know the truth of ourselves, we cannot truly know that which surrounds us. Technology in the hands of Self-ignorant men threatens the precious and delicately balanced natural environment upon which all life depends. As it stands now, our world hovers on the brink. However, there is light on the horizon.

Capitalism and cronyism in government is based on the 'me' principle; it is a projection of the ego. We see the results: an ever-increasing accumulation of wealth and power at the top; ever-increasing turmoil and despair at the bottom. The middle class finds itself squeezed at both ends, with its collective strength declining.

*'This is the way the world ends This is the way the world ends
This is the was the world ends Not with a bang but a wimper.'*
—*The Hollow Men*, T.S. Eliot (1888–1965)

A different system such as, for example, Cooperatism—of which the highly successful Mondragon experiment in the Basque region of Spain is a good example—must ultimately come to the fore if we are to survive as a civilization. However, such a system will succeed only if there is a shift away from 'me'-ness. Any true, positive and lasting change must be accompanied by an inner transformation on a global scale. Our global economic illness is fundamentally a spiritual illness. Real cooperation demands purity of intent; it is a state of Consciousness. Not everyone is ready for it, hence, unnecessary suffering continues.

We have a fundamental choice about how to be in the world. We can commit ourselves to making the world either a sweeter or a more bitter place for both human and other life forms. How we conduct ourselves in daily life is the external evidence of our inner choice. Delight is superior to wealth, but the two are not opposed. Let the world be, and be kind.

A Vision for Society

The Sage speaks:

'In a society consisting of followers of diverse ways of life, society is like the body and the members like its limbs. A member prospers by working for the good of society like a limb serving the body.

Through mind, speech and body one should always conduct oneself so as to serve the interests of society and should also awaken his circle to do likewise.

One should build up one's own circle so as to serve the interests of society and then make it prosper so that the society itself may prosper.

Society should be raised through *Shakti* (power) and then

Shanti (Peace) [is] established.

Brotherhood based on a sense of equality is the supreme goal to be attained by human society as a whole.

> *Through brotherhood, supreme peace will prevail amongst mankind and then this entire planet will flourish like a single household.*
> —*Sri Ramana Gita,* as spoken by Ramana Maharshi

'Shantih shantih shantih'
('Peace peace peace')

The last three words of *The Wasteland* by T.S. Eliot.

PART 3

THE PRIMACY OF CONSCIOUSNESS
An Essay on the Composition of Experience

'The Self, the true Consciousness of Shiva, shines as endless space within my Heart, as my very existence, beyond the reach of objective knowledge.'

—Sri Muruganar (1893–1973)

Experience Predicates Existence

The starting point of human understanding is the indisputable fact of *experience*. Experience is the *alpha* and *omega* of our earthly life. The content* of experience, whether truth or illusion, does not alter the fact that experience exists. There is experience, therefore, there is existence—experience predicates existence. What exists is experience and its contents—experience is constituted of content.

The meaning of the word experience is not delimited to my experience or even your experience, which is what common sense unconsciously assumes. The possessive adjective 'my' is a qualification mentally superimposed upon an impersonal substratum of experience. In fact, impersonal experience, where there is neither subject nor object, functions at a more fundamental level than the persona—the 'I-other' experience with which we are familiar.

Rather, it is an awareness of being—a being that is neither a thing nor not a thing, but rather an 'is-ness'. Outside direct experience, any other mode of existence is subject to doubt. We may infer that something exists beyond our immediate experience, but we can never prove it beyond all doubt. If you and I were to meet face to face, all we would know indubitably about each other is what we directly experience in that meeting. Upon parting, we would each undoubtedly assume the continued existence of the other even though no longer within range of the senses. Such assumptions however, are not indubitable.

Beyond direct experience, there is necessarily an element of

---

*In the sense of 'awareness of———'

doubt about the continued existence of what has been experienced. If we are not experiencing something directly, how can we be certain it exists? Others may testify that it does exist and we may hear it directly from their own lips, but how do we know that their testimony is still valid at the current moment when it is being uttered? And even though we experience the same object or person again and again, we have no guarantee that a further reappearance will occur.

Impersonal Experience Is 'Something-ness'

It is evident that the starting point for a description of the world—a description which includes the idea of the Self—is a ground of indeterminate and unqualified experience, most accurately characterized by the word 'something-ness'. The term 'something-ness' does not presuppose the subject-object duality inherent in other terms such as 'thing-ness', 'my-ness' or 'other-ness'. The dualistic thought or feeling or conviction that 'I' am the experiencer experiencing something other than myself rests upon a non-dualistic foundation of impersonal experience.

Indeterminate Experience Is Composed of Impressions

While it is evident that experience in its differentiated state is composed of objects and events standing in relation to an experiencing 'I'-subject, experience in its indeterminate state is present as a mass of unrelated impressions[*] that precede any sense of an observing or experiencing ego-self. Consider, for example, those occasions between sleeping and waking when there is consciousness of movement, sound, colour, etc., yet all is incomprehensible. There is a sense of 'am-ness' but no sense of a personal 'I', and nothing is familiar or has relatedness.

Rather, there is simply an impersonal awareness that

---

*Impressions: indeterminate, unrelated occurrences having no discernible cause.

something is happening. Similarly, those advanced in the practice of deep meditation note that there is a moment (or moments) between the thinking state of ordinary consciousness and the transcendent state of pure Consciousness in which something indeterminate is appearing, but not to a thinking or apprehending subject. In this state, the subject-as-locus has disappeared while an impersonal, non-local 'witness' remains. This witness is actually the unbounded Self (*Atman*) of Yoga.

The Notion of 'Sense-data' is Inferred

In fact, before the universe of subject and objects as the dominant content comes into being, experience in its primal form manifests as undifferentiated raw data which we have termed, 'impressions'.

We utilize the word 'impressions' to avoid the presumption of five physical senses feeding sense-data to the mind. The notion of senses feeding data is in actuality an inference which makes up an important part of our description of the world. It also explains to a large degree how we make up this description. Nevertheless, an inference is a conceptual assumption rather than a direct experience and is therefore subject to doubt. Impressions themselves cannot be doubted as they are simply what is being presented in consciousness.

For the present, therefore, we will presuppose nothing and accept only what is immediately present and unformulated. It is this early undeveloped stage of experience which establishes the fact of existence, for in the absence of these unformulated impressions, there can be no experience and ipso facto, no positing of existence, either a priori or a posteriori.

Experience Predicates Consciousness

Where there is experience, there is necessarily consciousness—experience predicates consciousness. In the absence of consciousness, there can be no experience, as in the state of deep sleep when consciousness gives way to unconsciousness and, simultaneously, experience disappears. In fact, we could argue that experience is consciousness undergoing apparent modifications while remaining what it is, i.e. consciousness.

Consciousness is the Ground of Experience

Unformulated impressions are not objects, nor is there any self-conscious subject apprehending them. They comprise undifferentiated experience (something-ness) and cannot be distinguished, in any conceptual sense, from consciousness.

Furthermore, while experience is consciousness, the converse is not necessarily true, i.e. consciousness is not always experience. Thus, the two terms are not tautological since while experience predicates consciousness, consciousness does not predicate experience. In other words, consciousness is the ultimate ground of all experience, not the converse.

Reality of Pure Consciousness Established by Vedanta

The various systems of Yoga have established that through meditation, it is possible to attain a state of pure consciousness, i.e. one void of impressions. The Sanskrit term for this state is *nirvikalpa samadhi*, meaning consciousness without qualities or, alternatively, consciousness without any form of appearance.

Nirvikalpa samadhi is a state that transcends both the conscious state of experience and the unconscious state of deep sleep. A precise definition of this and related states of consciousness has been succinctly worked out in the major texts of *advaita* Vedanta, as well as in Patanjali's *Yoga Sutras*, a treatise predating Christ and the most authoritative work of Yoga philosophy and practice.

Consciousness is the Ultimate Ground of All Phenomena

Impressions, which have their being in consciousness, are the foundation of all empirical knowledge. Experience, in the form of indeterminate impressions, is the primal manifestation of consciousness: a manifestation that is prerequisite to consciousness becoming intuitively—as distinct from conceptually—self-aware. Consciousness is the ground and support of impressions and, in turn, impressions are the ground of a world of objects and events of which one has to be conscious.

Consciousness-impressions

Impressions and consciousness, as inseparable constituents of experience, together constitute the ground of a determinate world-appearance. Their relationship, within the context of experience, is one of identity. Impressions have no being independent of consciousness, but rather have their being as appearing. As such, they are more accurately referred to as consciousness-impressions.

The Intuition of Consciousness Precedes its Concept

In the primal condition of non-dual indeterminate experience, there is neither an observing subject nor an observed object. The consciousness is also not conceptually self-aware, i.e. as the thought, 'I am conscious'; rather, consciousness subsists as an unbroken unity, free of the observer-observed duality. As established by Vedanta, consciousness will persist with or without the impressions, but in order for the intuition or awareness of consciousness to arise, there must be some alternating between the two states of consciousness-impressions and consciousness-by-itself, i.e. without impressions. How is this? Simply put by analogy, in order to know darkness, one must know its opposite, light, and in order to know light, one must know darkness. It is the juxtaposition of the two which creates awareness of the principle of light.

Similarly, it is the appearance and disappearance of impressions, occuring at the crossover between waking and sleeping, which produces the intuition of consciousness. Being awake means being conscious, regardless of the constantly changing contents of experience. When the contents of experience disappear with the onset of deep sleep, consciousness does too.

Upon awakening, there is a brief moment of consciousness-by-itself or pure consciousness (the *nirvikalpa samadhi* of deep meditation) followed immediately by consciousness-impressions. It is this juxtaposition which gives rise to the intuition (as distinct from concept) of consciousness. The concept of consciousness arises with the crossover from consciousness-impressions to consciousness-of-things.

The Notion of 'I Am'

Consciousness revealed through impressions is immediate undefined awareness without an object—it is consciousness-of-somethingness; it is not conceptual. Experience in the form of undifferentiated impressions incorporates the intuition of both consciousness and existence. It is this primal non-conceptual revelation which serves as the basis for the subsequent birth of the notion of an experiencing 'I' or subject.

The twin concepts of existence and consciousness arise as later developments following the birth of conceptual self-awareness in the form of the thought-feeling, 'I am'. This self-aware 'I am' personalizes the awareness of existence and consciousness as 'I exist' and 'I am conscious'. Thus, the intuitions of existence and consciousness which were pre-thoughts now take form conceptually as, 'I am, therefore I exist' and 'I am, therefore I am conscious.'

'I Am' is the Locus of The World-appearance

The thought, 'I am' is the primal thought of the phenomenal universe. Without it, there is no possibility of formulating a description of the world, for the world-appearance is a complex of objects and events which demand an observer and a locus in order to be known. This observer/locus is 'I am'. Neither the observer nor the observed can come into being independently. They are mutually dependent, for without a locus, there are no observed objects and without an object, there is no observing locus. The observer and the observed necessarily arise together as a mutually dependent subject-object dyad, in which the subject is the locus and objects make up its environment.

Existence and Consciousness are Inferred

Indeterminate simple impressions are a necessary yet insufficient condition for notions of consciousness and existence to arise. Although consciousness and existence are revealed by the contents of experience, they cannot be directly observed. Not being directly observed, they are inferred. Their inference is analogous to the inference of light. No observer actually sees light, only colour. However, in the absence of light, there can be no colour. When there is light, there can be colour and it is through the experience of colour that light is inferred. Similarly, no one actually sees either consciousness or existence, only objects, whether gross (sensory) or subtle (ideas, memories, etc.). In their absence, there can be no objects, impressions or any other form of experience. When they are present, there can be objects, and it is through objective experience that both consciousness and existence are not merely intuited, but inferred conceptually. However, any inference requires both a thinking subject and an object of thought. Therefore, the birth of the ego or empirical self ('I am') is the sufficient condition for the notions of consciousness and existence.

The inferences of consciousness and existence are unlike the ordinary inferences of daily life. When we see smoke rising from behind a hill, we will infer fire even though we do not see it directly. In all probability, our inference will be confirmed once we take a look behind the hill. But not necessarily. The smoke could turn out to be steam rising from the boilers of a factory.

We know that these ordinary inferences are mere probabilities, whereas inferences of consciousness and existence are of a different order, i.e. they cannot be inferred directly from the data of the senses, as in the case of smoke and fire.

Consciousness and existence are not perceivable objects or events and we cannot confirm them empirically. Rather, they are of the nature of principles or ideas. We must assume them as a priori truths, in the absence of which knowledge in any form would be impossible. Just as the visual appearance of a tree in the absence of light is inconceivable, equally inconceivable is the appearance of a thought or an object in the absence of either consciousness or existence. Inferences of consciousness and existence are a priori, whereas ordinary inferences, such as fire from smoke, are a posteriori. Ordinary inferences presuppose a causal connection (e.g., fire causes smoke) which may prove wrong. However, the priori inferences of consciousness and existence are the indisputable presuppositions of all experience, since in the absence of the former there is no possibility of the latter nor can the question of causality arise.

The thought-feeling of subjectivity ('I am') is a condition sufficient for the notions of consciousness and existence to arise, which take explicit form as the cognitions, 'I am conscious' and

'I exist'. These cognitions are implicit in all cognitions of the subject-object form, such as 'I am touching this chair'. The very statement, 'I am touching this chair' asserts existence and consciousness in both a personal atomic form ('I exist', 'I am conscious') and an impersonal universal form ('there is existence', 'there is consciousness'). In fact, it is this act of cognition which upholds and reinforces the thought, 'I am', and which affirms the axiomatic notions of consciousness and existence.

No Proof That Impressions Have a Cause

Experience originates as simple consciousness-impressions. What is the cause of these impressions? We cannot say with certainty, since they are the most fundamental level of experience accessible to us. There is nothing in our direct experience which points undeniably to their cause or even proves they have a cause. Any theory we come up with, such as the theory that impressions are caused by a material, external world (which includes the physical senses) either impinging on or creating consciousness, must always remain a possibility since such a world is an inferred world and not one which we can know directly or prove absolutely. Thus, the world that we do know without qualification is the world of experience itself and not any other world.

And so we are left with the intriguing question: 'Does anything exist beyond experience itself?' This is one of the oldest and most debated questions of philosophy. For the present, however, we will leave this topic aside and focus instead on how the world-appearance is brought into being.

Subject and Object are Mutually Dependent

In the absence of impressions, as in deep sleep (unconsciousness) or *nirvikalpa samadhi* (pure consciousness), there is no experience of something-ness and therefore no possibility of a sense of subjectivity. Furthermore, without a determinate thing arising from the indeterminate ground of somethingness, there can be no awareness of an experiencing subject. It is not the impressions themselves that give rise to the subjective sense, but rather the objects and events that are formulated from impressions.

With the birth of the object comes, simultaneously, the birth of the subject, and vice versa. Object and subject are not entities separated by time and distance, nor does one cause the other—rather, they are born, coexist and disappear together. An object is any cognition of, for example, a concept, a memory or a physical entity, such as a tree. Any moment or act of cognition points in two directions simultaneously—one at the object, the other at the subject. It is only with the co-arrival of the subjective sense of I-ness and the objective sense of otherness that conceptions of consciousness and existence, i.e. 'I am conscious', 'I exist', are cognized. These cognitions are themselves subtle objects (ideas) coexisting with the sense of subjectivity ('I am'). These subtle objects require a subject, i.e. they point to a cognizer. Equally, the cognizing subject requires an object, i.e. it points to what is cognized.

Since both subtle and gross objects of cognition are continually appearing and transforming (either by subtle modification or by radical change), it is easy to make the mistake of assuming a stable discrete subject who is experiencing a stream of unfolding events. This sense of an enduring, atomic subject is illusory, since at the moment in which all objective content disappears (as with the onset of deep sleep or the attainment of *nirvikalpa samadhi*), all sense of subjectivity disappears as well, thus putting into question the assertion of a persisting, independent locus of experience, i.e. subject, ego or empirical self. The subject must have an object in order to be self-aware. With the disappearance of objectivity, self-awareness vanishes too. Consciousness may remain, resting in its own luminosity, as in the case of *nirvikalpa samadhi*, but there will be no awareness of a discrete 'I', i.e. observer, experiencer, knower, thinker, etc.

No Proven Cause for the 'Subject-Object' Dyad

Since subject and object arise simultaneously, having therefore no causal relationship, we must consider the possibility of an alternative causal factor or impetus which gives rise to this dyad. One such possibility, for example, could be a biologically driven urge in a newborn to survive. Such an innate, biological programme could trigger a sense of I-ness simultaneously with an awareness of the mother's breast as the means of survival. Such a hypothesis, however, presupposes an external material reality underlying all appearance. Such a supposition is an inference and, admittedly, a very powerful one, but it does not have the absolute certainty of direct experience. All such theories legitimately fall into the domain of the empirical sciences, to be alternatively validated, modified or rejected through further research, and all such theories—however credible—remain subject to doubt.

Objects are Configurations of Impressions

Having put forward the proposition that consciousness-impressions are the indeterminate ground from which the determinate subject-object dyad emerges, we will examine more closely how impressions are transformed into objects. An impression is any specific data that, when collocated with other specific data produces differentiation in an otherwise indeterminate field of somethingness. Impressions form the raw data that constitute objects. Objects are complexes of impressions—configurations which take form in consciousness and are revealed as phenomena.

The various collocations of impressions constitute, collectively, the complex universe of objects and events which we know. This world-appearance includes, necessarily, both the objective and subjective aspects of experience, since all objects of knowledge exist in relation to a knowing subject. The world-appearance necessarily includes an empirical locus or subject, since it is impossible to even imagine a universe except from the point of view of a subject which is located somewhere and sometime within that same universe.

Impressions Become the 'Qualities' Of Objects

With the birth of objects arrives the naming of different categories of impressions—the major categories being the five types of sense-data, specifically colours (seeing), sounds (hearing), tactile sensations (touching), flavours (tasting) and odours (smelling).

Terms such as 'hard', 'salty', 'blue', 'screech', etc. are names given to specific impressions which are members of these five categories of sense. The names given to impressions are themselves subtle objects (ideas) which serve to distinguish specific impressions from the indeterminate mass of somethingness to which they belong. Once we give a name to an impression, we turn it into something it hitherto was not, i.e. a quality (e.g., hot, sweet, blue, etc.), and this can occur only after the subject-object duality has arisen. Furthermore, in their indeterminate state, impressions cannot be singled out and named until a number of them have been collocated into an object, such as a chair. These collocated impressions become objectified and named once they are recognized as belonging to a larger, complex whole, i.e. object or event, perceived by a cognizing subject.

All the various names we can give to impressions fall into a general category called 'qualities', and qualities exist by virtue of belonging to objects and events and their relations. The world of our experience is a composition composed of impressions which have been transformed into the now determinate qualities of objects and events which make up our description of the universe. Each of these qualities is given a name, as are the objects and events which they comprise—what Indian philosophy calls *namarupa*, i.e. the world of name and form.

Objects Infer But Do Not Prove an External World

Once a group of impressions are collocated they are known collectively as an object or event which, generally, is regarded by common sense as having a substantial, independent existence. Through this process the object manifests as an apparent material reality quite distinct from the knowing subject. Common sense also assumes that this material reality exists independently of the knower. In fact, however, these collocations are essentially interpretations drawn from an indeterminate ground of impressions and, as with any interpretation, they are subject to doubt. Thus, the same collocation of impressions that at one moment is interpreted as 'snake' may a moment later be reinterpreted as 'rope'.

Once a group of impressions are configured or objectified, these hitherto unnamed, indeterminate, immaterial, simple elements of experience are transformed into the named, differentiated, material qualities of an object. In this way, our objects become increasingly reified; that is to say, they solidify as apparently discrete material entities, quite distinct from and independent of the knowing subject to whom, in truth, they belong.

Time and Space as Contexts for Change and Form

Along with this process of configuration and reification of the various phenomena comes awareness of change and form in their respective contexts of time and space—change occurring in time, and form occurring in space. A chair, for example, is a phenomenon which in the very act of creation is given duration and extension, as well as location, somewhere and sometime within the general contexts of time and space.

Time and space, as contexts, are not visible yet are inferred through observation of changing states and relations pertaining to objects and events. So long as the phenomenon 'chair' is held in awareness, the chair exists; should this interpretation cease, 'chair' will dissolve back into the elements from which it was configured. The appearance 'chair' is a configuration superimposed upon the underlying, indeterminate ground of consciousness-impressions.

Nevertheless, it now appears as a materially solid and independent object laid on the original flux. Thus, all the objective phenomena of the world-appearance, from the furthest galaxies to the minutiae of the organism, from what is exterior to what is interior to the observer, are configured from and rest upon this indeterminate ground.

Experience and Knowledge Not Different from Consciousness

This conclusion is not to be confused with solipsism, which asserts that nothing exists beyond the contents of the mind. Here we are saying that what exists beyond any doubt is experience, the content of which—including the idea of the self or subject—is not different from consciousness. Beyond experience, there may or may not be other independent, existing things, but these will never be known directly and positively for knowledge itself is of the nature of experience and therefore consciousness. Knowledge of an apparently independent, external thing (such as a chair) is not the Kantian 'thing-in-itself', and if we try to assert that knowledge of a thing is the 'thing-in-itself', then that thing is neither independent nor external to the knowing consciousness.

However compelling the inference that experience reveals the existence of a reality independent of consciousness, such independence must remain forever a mere possibility since it can never be directly verified. Besides hypothesis and inference, there is no bridge between experience and a reality external to experience. Indirect verification through inference at best presents an arguable case for an external, material universe, but never proof.

The notion of external reality has heuristic value with regard to the physical sciences. It is this heuristic principle that allows for the development of technology and continued research at all levels—from the microscopic to the macrocosmic. Nevertheless, while science or philosophy may posit a material universe standing outside of consciousness and functioning in some sort of structural and dynamic correspondence to the world of our direct experience, this will never be proven absolutely; and while it is useful for practical purposes to work with this hypothesis, it is invalid to regard it as an unassailable truth.

The Primacy of Consciousness

In this essay, I have endeavoured to show that impressions are the manifest ground of the world-appearance. However, due to the fact that our daily experience is dominated by the perception of objects and their relations, this underlying ground of indeterminate impressions is easily overlooked. We assume that what we are seeing, hearing or touching is the thing itself, rather than a collocation of consciousness-impressions appearing as matter, i.e. name and form (*namarupa*).

We have shown that impressions have no independent existence and that, indeed, they are not different from consciousness. For this reason, we have stated that impressions are more accurately termed, consciousness-impressions. Additionally, we have pointed out that while consciousness is a necessary condition for impressions, impressions are not a necessary condition for consciousness. Consciousness will persist without or with impressions, as has been established through the ancient and well-documented systems of Yoga and Vedanta. Practitioners of these systems have consistently testified to the accessibility of pure consciousness (*nirvikalpa samadhi*)—a state free from impressions, thoughts or any form of appearance.

I have also argued that impressions, as the fundamental constituents of experience, predicate both existence and consciousness. There are impressions, therefore there is existence, i.e. the existence of impressions. Furthermore, since impressions represent the most fundamental level of direct experience apart from consciousness itself, it is impossible to prove beyond any doubt whether their existence has been caused by something external to consciousness. External causes may be inferred, but all such inferential knowledge is unproven.

What can be affirmed, without doubt, is the being of impressions and the being of consciousness. The appearance of impressions predicates both consciousness and existence, not as a duality, but as a unity; that is, consciousness and existence are two terms for the same thing. I have also pointed out that impressions cannot manifest in the absence of consciousness, whereas consciousness exists with or without impressions. And this leads us, finally, to the conclusion that consciousness itself, being indisputable, is the certain ground of all experiences, thereby giving it primacy over all other possibilities.

AUM TAT SAT
(Supreme Absolute Truth)

Jai Hind

BIBLIOGRAPHY

Sastry, Alladi Mahadeva (trans.). 1995. *'The Bhagavad-Gita'* with *Commentary of Sri Sankaracharya*. Madras: Samata Books.

Berkeley, George. *A Treatise Concerning The Principles of Human Knowledge*, Dublin: Trinity-College.

Bohm, David. 2002. *Wholeness and the Implicate Order*. London: Routledge Classics.

Swami, B.V. Narasimha. 2002. *Self-Realization: Life and Teachings of Ramana Maharshi*. Tiruvannamalai: V.S. Ramanan.

Capra, Fritjof. 1999. *The Tao of Physics*. Boston: Shambala Publications.

Sankaracharya, Sri. 1983. *Crest-Jewel of Wisdom*, trans. Mohini Chatterji. Madras: Theosophical Publishing House.

Dyczkowski, Mark S. G. 1987. *The Doctrine of Vibration: An Analysis of the Doctrines and Practices of Kashmir Shaivism*. Albany: State University of New York.

1994. *E.E. Cummings: Complete Poems, 1904–1962*, edited by George James Firmage. W.W. Norton & Company.

Dasgupta, Surendranath. 1992. *A History of Indian Philosophy*. Delhi: Motilal Banarsidass.

Descartes, Rene. 1637. *Discourse On Method*.

Eliot, T.S. 1963. *T.S. Eliot: Collected Poems 1909–1962*. London: Faber and Faber.

Frawley, Dr David (Pandit Vamadeva Shastri). 1991. *Gods, Sages and*

Kings: Vedic Secrets of Ancient Civilization. Utah: Passage Press.

Frawley, Dr David (Pandit Vamadeva Shastri). 2000. *Vedantic Meditation: Lighting the Flame of Awareness*. Berkeley: North Atlantic Books.

Gambhirananda, Swami (trans.). 2004. '*Brahma Sutra Bashya of Sankaracharya*'. Advaita Ashrama.

2000. *The Power of the Presence: Transforming Encounters with Sri Ramana Maharshi* edited by David Godman. Boulder: Avadhuta Foundation.

Goswami, Amit. 1995. *The Self-Aware Universe: How Consciousness Creates the Material World*. New York: Penguin Putnam Inc.

Hegel, Georg. 1977. *Phenomenology Of Spirit*, trans. A.V. Miller. Oxford: Oxford University Press.

Heidegger, Martin. 1944-45. *Country Path Conversations,* trans. Bret W. Davis Bloomington. Indiana: Indiana University Press.

Hume, David. 1740. *A Treatise Of Human Nature.*

Sankaracharya, Sri. 1941. *A Thousand Teachings*, trans. Swami Jagadananda. Madras: Sri Ramakrishna Math.

Kant, Immanuel. 1781. *The Critique of Pure Reason.*

Lakshmanjoo, Swami, & John Hughes. 2001. *Shiva Sutras: The Supreme Awakening*. Culver: Universal Shaiva Fellowship.

Madhavananda, Swami (trans.). 1993. '*The Brhadranayaka Upanishad*' with Commentary of Sri Sankaracharya. Calcutta: Advaita Ashrama.

Vidyaranya, Madhava. 1986. *Sankara Digvijaya*: *The Traditional Life of Sri Sankarcharya*, trans. Swami Tapasyananda. Madras: Sri Ramakrishna Math.

Milton, John. 2008. *L'Allegro and Il Penseroso 1608–74*. BiblioBazaar.

2004. *Padamalai*, trans. & edited by David Godman, T.V. Venkatasubramanian & Robert Butler. Boulder: Avadhuta Foundation.

The Collected Works of Sri Ramana Maharishi edited by Arthur Osborne. Tamil Nadu: Sri Ramanasramam Tiruvannamalai.

Popper, Karl. 1992. *The Logic of Scientific Discovery*. London: Routledge.

1975. *The Upanishads: Breath of the Eterna,* trans. Swami Prabhavananda, & Frederick Manchester; New York.

1995. *The Ribhu Git,* trans. Dr H. Ramamoorthy.

2000. *Talks With Ramana Maharshi: On Realizing Abiding Peace and Happine.* Carlsbad: Inner Directions Publishing.

Russell, Bertrand. 1966. *Our Knowledge of the External World.* London: Routledge.

———. 2007. *The Problems of Philosophy.* Cosimo Classics.

———. 1961. *Religion And Science.* Oxford: Oxford University Press.

Sartre, Jean-Paul. 1943. *Being And Nothingness: An Essay on Phenomenological Ontology.*

Schrodinger, Erwin. 1964. *My View of the World.* Cambridge: Cambridge University Press.

Spinoza, Benedict de. 2005. *Ethics,* trans. Edwin Curley. Penguin Classics.

Sarma, Sri K. Lakshmana. 2002. *Maha Yoga.* Tamil Nadu: Sri Ramanasramam, Tiruvannamalai.

Stanford, Jim. 2008. *Economics For Everyone: A Short Guide To The Economics Of Capitalism.* Pluto Press.

Thévenaz, Pierre. 1965. *What Is Phenomenology?* Chicago: Quadrangle Books.

Venkatesananda, Swami. 1984. *The Concise Yoga Vasistha.* Albany: State University of New York Press.

2004. *Sri Ramana Gita,* trans. Swami Visvanatha, Sri, Prof. K. Swaminathan. Sri Nithyanada Printers.

Wittgenstein, Ludwig. 1994. *Tractatus Logico-Philosophicus,* trans. D.F. Pears and B.F. McGuinness. Routledge & Kegan Paul.

www.ingramcontent.com/pod-product-compliance
Lightning Source LLC
Chambersburg PA
CBHW030233170426
43201CB00006B/199